Walk with the Lord

Advent-Christmas

SHARING THE SILENCE, SHARING THE LIFE

by
Fr. Anselm W. Romb, OFM Conv.

St. Paul Books & Media

Library of Congress Cataloging-in-Publication Data

Romb, Anselm W. (Anselm William), 1929-
    Walk with the Lord : Sharing the silence, sharing the life / by
Anselm W. Romb.
        p.   cm.
    ISBN 0-8198-8245-3 : $6.95
    1. Advent—Meditations.   2. Christmas—Meditations.   3. Epiphany
season—Meditations.   4. Penance—Meditations.   5. Catholic Church—
Prayer-books and devotions—English.   I. Title.
BX2170.A4R65   1990
242'.33—dc20   90-44397
                                                                    CIP

All scripture selections in *italicized* type are taken from *The New American Bible with Revised New Testament* Copyrighted © 1986 by the Confraternity of Christian Doctrine, Washington, D.C., and are used with permission. All rights reserved. Other scripture selections or references to scriptural texts are those of the author.

Printed and published in the U.S.A. by St. Paul Books & Media
50 St. Paul's Ave., Boston, MA 02130

St. Paul Books & Media is the publishing house of the Daughters of St. Paul, an international congregation of women religious serving the Church with the communications media.

2 3 4 5 6 7 8 9   98 97 96 95 94 93 92 91

This book is dedicated to all those priests and laity
who taught me to love the Word of God
and encouraged me both to preach and to write.
Generous affirmation and honest criticism
are the pillars on which the pulpit rests.

Contents

Advent Season

First Week of Advent 13
Solemnity of the Immaculate Conception. 37
Second Week of Advent 41
Third Week of Advent 61
Fourth Sunday of Advent 81
December 17-24 91

Christmas Season

Christmas 109
Holy Family—Sunday in the Octave of Christmas 113
December 26-31 117
January 1—Solemnity of Mary, Mother of God 131
Second Sunday after Christmas 135
Epiphany 139
January 2-12 or Weekdays following Epiphany 143
The Baptism of the Lord—Sunday after January 6 171

Appendix

Preparation for the Sacrament of Reconciliation, I 177
Preparation for the Sacrament of Reconciliation, II . . . 179
Preparation for the Sacrament of Reconciliation, III . . . 181

PREFACE

For those who use these scriptural and liturgical reflections, I suggest reading the Bible texts on which they are based.

These reflections have multiple uses. They are principally for laypersons' daily meditations during the two liturgical seasons mentioned in the title. Secondly, those religious, clerics, and laypersons who pray the daily Office may wish to substitute these reflections for the second reading of the Office of Readings, although they derive from the weekday and Sunday texts of the Mass.

Preachers who are accustomed to preach every day during the cycles of Advent and Christmas may find this book a source of ideas. Because these commentaries would generally be too long, the preacher can readily choose those ideas which will generate a homily of suitable length.

Included also are some preparations for Penitential Services during Advent that may prove helpful for all readers.

My thanks to Terrie Huizinga of Rockford, MI, for her professional help in typing this manuscript on computer disk. Without her I could not have completed this work.

Fr. Anselm W. Romb, OFM Conv.

Advent
Season

FIRST WEEK OF ADVENT

First Sunday
of Advent, A

Is 2:1-5;
Rom 13:11-14; Mt 24:37-44

The word "advent" derives from the Latin for "coming" or "arrival." But Advent is actually a time for "going," for "departure." Advent is a pilgrimage and the Bible is the travelog outlining God's faithfulness to his journeying people. Advent summarizes in four weeks the four thousand years during which the people of God, the Israelites, waited for the Savior and Messiah. Through the patriarchs, prophets and kings, God called his people to national consciousness so as to provide the matrix of our salvation.

We are called, like the Jews of old and the primitive Christian community, to detach ourselves from the familiar ways of sin, comfortable laziness, the rigidity of our own opinions and ways of doing things. We are committing ourselves to a journey of faith.

The implications of pilgrimage are several. We are not tied down to one place on this earth. We detach ourselves from what is secure and predictable. We are willing to make as many fresh starts as necessary to progress. We try to hear the voice of the Lord over the distractions of this world. To be a pilgrim means to be on the move, on the way to the kingdom.

Sometimes, however, we are seduced into becoming a tourist instead. Whereas the pilgrim seeks the mountain of God and his sanctuary, the tourist's objective is diversion, pleasure and a frequent change of pace. Is it not true that many a believer is more tourist than pilgrim? While a tourist sunbathes and has a cocktail, choosing ease and indulgence, the pilgrim climbs over the next hill with a road map, studying the Bible and reinforcing his or her prayer life.

Isaiah seeks the unity of nations under God. He tells the nations to let go of their past, their warfare, their exploitation of others. Paul, in a practical way, begins with family, friends and neighbors. In Romans, Paul tells us to come out of the dark, where evil deeds are done and give up carousing, lust and jealousy. The vices he names are what divide us: carousing, sexual excess and envy of others. We use others, try to get one up on others, resort to violent words and actions. These are "small murders," taking "pot shots" at others. Yet the Christian life is not complex. Rather, it involves discharging the duties of our state in life, doing an honest day's work, using the gifts God has given us.

Therefore, look upon Advent as a serious undertaking and a time of getting your affairs in order: foreseeing the occasions of temptation and sin, giving spiritual goals priority and paying whatever price is necessary to make the grade up the mountain of God.

Ask yourself some pertinent questions: Have you studied the road maps, the words of Jesus? Do you recognize the road signs, the teachings of the Church? Are you in good health for traveling, with a solid prayer life and the spirit of sacrifice? Have you consulted the persons who know the way, such as your pastor, confessor, spiritual director, spiritual authors? Above all, do you really want to travel?

In the Gospel, Jesus remarks about the pair of men working in the field and the women grinding meal: one will be taken and one will be left. It is not hard to figure out who were the pilgrims and who the tourists. These four weeks are a gift from God. They are a time to think about the important issues in life, even though at the end of Advent it may seem that our travel and waiting were in vain. Sometimes Jesus does not come in the way we expect, or to some it may seem he never arrives. That is why the primary lesson of Advent is not the coming of Christmas, but learning to wait for the visitation of the Lord when and how he decides to reveal himself clearly.

In seeking out the words of Jesus in the Bible, always begin with the original text. If you have various Bibles at hand, compare the differing translations. Although the Bible is the basis for Christian doctrine, its purpose is not simply to inform us, but to transform us. Our search for the "real" Jesus will not be over until we meet the Bible's principal author face to face. Then, our transformation will be complete and our pilgrimage over. It is said that a book should be read only as carefully as it was written.... God wrote his book very carefully, indeed!

First Sunday
of Advent, B

Is 63:16-17, 19; 64:2-7;
1 Cor 1:3-9; Mk 13:33-37

Anticipation of a future event often brings greater joy than the actual event. Our longing for Christmas, however, is mixed with contrition for sin and the good resolutions that accompany a beginning—in this case, the beginning of the liturgical year. In the first reading, Isaiah conveys a sense of urgency. *"Oh, that you would rend the heavens and come down,... Would that you might meet us doing right....*" Then he poignantly adds, "*Yet, O LORD, you are our father; we are the clay and you the potter: we are all the work of your hands.*"

In comparison with the Jewish people, to whom the full nature of God was an unrevealed mystery, it is easy for us who have known and seen Jesus, at least through the Gospels, to long for the return which he has promised. With the psalmist we can say, "*If your face shine upon us, then we shall be safe*" (Ps 80:20). An important dimension of waiting for the Lord's visitation, which can come at any time, is silence, quiet time and seclusion, wherein God can soften your heart, empty your mind of transitory goals and separate you from hidden personal agendas.

At a time of the year when only a few leaves bravely cling to their branches, Isaiah laments (and we with him), "*We have all withered like leaves, and our guilt carries us away like the wind.*" This is not necessarily because we are such inveterate sinners. Nevertheless, we must judge every sin not merely according to the acts or omissions themselves, but according to the graces we have rejected. That is why the saints could accurately label themselves the worst of sinners, because their graces were so significant! But we are always in danger of complacency.

As we keep watch through the "purple" days of Advent, God is watching us—but not as the world, our bosses and even sometimes our family seem to observe us. God is not a spy playing a game of "gotcha!" We are so accustomed to surveillance that we could tend to see God in that light. Our phones are tapped; we are trapped by radar and watched by police helicopters. We are frisked at airport security, monitored by TV cameras in banks and supermarkets, have our credit checked by computers. God's vigil, on the other hand, is not meant to trap us, but to free us of sin, guilt and death.

We are thinking of the Infant Jesus of Christmas. But again in today's readings, the Church is presenting the long-range view: the Day of the Lord, the second coming of Jesus on judgment day. At his first coming, Jesus was a helpless child who grew up to be judged by the people of his time. At his second coming, Jesus will give judgment as a mighty king, manifesting his divinity, power and majesty. Millions have rejected the message of his first appearance, but nobody can escape his final one.

During this liturgical year, we shall follow the birth, ministry, death and glorification of the Lord. It is fitting, therefore, to place some questions before us now and review our answers from time to time throughout the whole year: Do I judge the magnitude of my sins by the graces I have been rejecting? Do Church holidays merely mean the relaxation of discipline with "fun and games," or do they mean entering into the mystery of Jesus? Am I willing to "let go" and allow God to be the potter and myself the clay? Do I make for myself a quiet time and space to be alone with the Lord? Is my fear of God filial, that is, childlike? Or do I cringe under the heavy hand of a taskmaster? Do I put off repentance, thinking that I still have plenty of time? Will I be ready for my particular judgment if I die during this liturgical year?

Submit to God. Receive him into your life today. Cry out with the psalmist, *"If your face shine upon us, then we shall be safe"* (Ps 80:20).

Turning to the Lord can be risky, but the best athletes generally get the worst bruises. Sometimes you have to plunge deeply and swallow water if you want to learn to swim. On the other hand, you can drown even close to shore through timidity, depression or the ignoring of rules.

First Sunday of Advent, C

Jer 33:14-16; 1 Thes 3:12—4:2;
Lk 21:25-28, 34-36

Despite the commercialism at this time of the year and our own traditional expectations of Christmas, none of the readings of Cycle A, B or C refer to the birth of Jesus. All the texts refer to the second coming of the Lord at the end of the world. That is why this season is so somber. The vestments are purple. There is less singing and fanfare; we omit the *Gloria*. Because today initiates the liturgical year, this is the time to take inventory and do accounting. That is, do your repenting early and avoid the Christmas rush. In contemporary language: Get your act together, because the *big scene* is coming sooner than we expect. There is a saying: "This is the first day of the rest of your life." But today is also the last day of your past life, the summation of your personal history. Do not be distressed at your slow growth and the drudgery of plodding forward. Your efforts are a sign of your loyalty to God.

The apocalyptic words of Jesus in the Gospel are not comforting. He tells us to pray mightily for strength to escape what lies ahead. When Paul tells the Thessalonians they had better make greater progress, he is saying that you can never stand still, mark time, expect to remain in the same place. You either go forward or you slip backwards.

Emotions are mixed about the end of the world. It is thought by some that Jesus will return when all the "places" in heaven vacated by the fallen angels are filled by human beings. So one would think we would want to hurry the endtime. But not very many persons seem to be yearning for the Day of the Lord—at least not in their own lifetime. After death it won't make any difference when the crack of doom sounds, because, as far as the dead are concerned, their end has come.

If a C.T.A. (Celestial Travel Agency), with a pair of angels, conducted a one-way tour into eternity, I suspect that the waiting lines would be short. We might hear reasons like the following from some potential travelers: "Yes, I want to take that trip, but what if I don't end up in heaven? Anyway, I have to 'convert' myself to Jesus better. I want to spend more time with my family, especially now that the children are growing up so fast. I want to get involved in church work or neighborhood groups, so I can make up for the bad things I've done. I will make up with that relative I have hated for so long; we haven't talked for years. I've never even read the Bible all the way through."

Actually, the only adequate response to such remarks is that everyone has to take that one-way trip sooner or later. There is no point in putting off the necessary changes in life. It is helpful to review the Gospel for today. *"Stand erect"* means to remember your dignity. You are a member of God's family, a soldier under his command, a temple of grace and glory. Stand up and be counted. *"Raise your heads"* means to lift your eyes and your mind to higher values than this world counsels. *"Beware"* of *"carousing"* (consumerism and commercialism), *"drunkenness"* (too much partying after work) and *"the anxieties of daily life"* (anxiety over your job, your future, your debts).

Remember the parable of the hireling who did not care about watching the sheep. Perhaps until now you had the mindset of a hireling: "That's not my job" and so you do the least. As a member of a "family-owned business" which is the Mystical Body of Christ, you are responsible for everyone else, but especially for those with whom you come in daily contact. If you were a hireling you acted for pay. That is, you went to church and were reasonably "good," making a deal with God who would then let you into heaven by the skin of your teeth. You were a hireling who lived, not out of love, but with fear of being "fired" by God and thrown into hell-fire.

Ask yourself these questions: Are you alarmed about your state of soul? What would you start doing if you had only one week to live? What judgment do you think is awaiting you? How long have you just "marked time" with no improvement in prayer, charity, honesty? When will you reverse those "hireling" trends in your life and join the family?

During the greeting of peace, perhaps we should wish each other a Happy New Year, because this is the start of the liturgical year, a time for initiatives, new projects and resolutions.

Monday of the First Week of Advent, A

Is 4:2-6;
Mt 8:5-11

Several elements of this touching gospel scene are striking. The human qualities attract our attention, excite our wonder and teach us a lesson. First, it is remarkable that an officer of the Roman army would be concerned about a servant "boy." The Latin and Greek texts use the words *puer* and *pais*, which imply that the "boy" was not the centurion's son, but his slave. Even older male slaves were called "boy" in ancient times because of their dependence on the master's orders.

When a slave was crippled or bedridden due to old age—in this Gospel, even paralyzed—it was not unusual for the typical owner to throw the useless, aged, handicapped and unprofitable slave into the streets, or to sell such a person to be used in some task that did not require mobility. Therefore, it is a wonder that the sick "boy" had won the affection of his master, the centurion, who must have been an honorable, even loving person. Jesus surely recognized the man's virtue.

A centurion was a "non-commissioned" officer, that is, someone not born into nobility, as were the higher officers. A centurion need not even be a Roman citizen. He was not born to command, but someone promoted from the lower ranks of conscripts or enlisted men, perhaps because of his bravery in the field or organizational ability. "Centurion" means "one hundred," but Roman divisions were seldom at full strength, so the centurion of this Gospel probably commanded seventy or eighty men. Jews were excused from military service for religious reasons, such as having to offer incense to the pagan gods during military campaigns and marching behind standards that were "graven images." This centurion was probably part of the Syrian army of occupation. Yet he was sensitive enough to realize that Jesus, a devout Jew, would not want to enter a Gentile house, lest he become ritually unclean. (In Luke's version of the story, chapter 5, Jesus is already on his way to the officer's house.)

The centurion points out to Jesus that his troops obey him without question. Indeed, obedience was the hallmark of the successful Roman army. His faith led him to believe that Jesus could likewise "command" his slave's illness at a distance. *"Only say the word and my servant will be healed."* This sentiment flowed from the first four verses of Matthew 8, which precede the centurion's plea. A leper was miraculously cured by Jesus' simply declaring, *"I will do it. Be made clean."* The officer's trust is a model for all ages.

Another point Matthew may have been making is that Gentiles were being admitted equally into Jesus' kingdom. Analogously, we who enjoy membership in the Church should be humbly grateful and show indulgence towards those without the gift of membership. We should also respect other religions and diverse theological positions of our fellow believers, although we need not agree, of course.

As we make our Advent pilgrimage, let us ask for healing for ourselves and those whom we cherish, just as the centurion did. Finally, let us ask for trust in the power of Jesus to enter our "house" and change our life and bring us in good health into his kingdom.

Faith, however, does not imply that we are "making deals" with God. Faith means doing the right thing because it is right. Failure, apart from any deliberate sin, doesn't displease God. Failure is a springboard to the next leap upward. In between the valleys and mountains, plateaus are the norm—the terrain that permits the safest and fastest travel.

Monday of the First Week of Advent, B, C

Is 2:1-5;
Mt 8:5-11

This reading is taken from chapter 2 of Isaiah, but chapter 1 sets the tone for his prophecies. From the outset, Isaiah reviews the wickedness of God's people. In the familiar metaphor of the Jewish and Christian Testaments, which liken the covenant between God and his people to a marriage contract, Jerusalem is called an adulteress, an unfaithful woman who consorts with false, foreign gods. Murderers abide within her walls and the leaders are comrades of thieves and seekers of bribes who ignore widows and orphans.

Judah, however, will be purified by the Lord and Jerusalem will again become a holy city. The threat of judgment is changed to words of comfort in chapter 2. Because of renewed fidelity to her Lord, foreigners will no longer occupy and control the holy city. Here we read the often-quoted Isaian text, *"They shall beat their swords into plowshares and their spears into pruning hooks; One nation shall not raise the sword against another, nor shall they train for war again."*

Peace is the great dream of mankind. Yet so much suffering results from the squandering of talents and resources on armaments. War causes people to be wounded and killed, orphaned and widowed, displaced, homeless and impoverished. The pride, ambition and greed of some leaders, their lust for power and the manipulation of others weaker than themselves, incite whole nations to battle. All reason cedes to the battle cry. If the same efforts and resources had been turned to humanitarian causes, poverty, hunger and ignorance would long ago have been abolished—and probably most disease as well. Military leaders try to glorify war with medals, monuments and autobiographies. They ornament weapons for killing. Better that farmers would goldplate their tractors and plumbers their wrenches. Food and plumbing are much more valuable to civilization than ammunition.

The ancient Romans had a proverb, *Si vis pacem, para bellum,* "If you want peace, prepare for war." This seems to be the justification for the arms race in our times. Pope Paul VI said, "If you want peace, work for justice." The ancient psalmist wrote, *"Justice and peace shall kiss"* (Ps 85:11).

Peace is not meant to be the quiet of a cemetery. Peace is the orderly and vibrant human exchange between men and women working in a free environment to complete creation and apply the effects of redemption, thus building the holy city, God's new Jerusalem. Peace, then, bespeaks harmony between human beings and creation, between human beings and God. Is this not simply a description of the primal earthly paradise where Adam walked with God as the perfectly natural thing to do and nature was neither exploited nor harmful? Adam and Eve were innocent and closely bonded. After the fall, Adam blamed Eve and she blamed the serpent. All harmony disappeared. Outside the garden Adam had to earn bread with heavy toil and Eve bore children with pain. Cain killed his own brother and sin proliferated among the human race. The sacred writer used these stories to account for mankind's unfortunate condition and to provide a theological explanation of evil in the world.

Nevertheless, we all look for a happy ending to a story, which, in fact, took place after thousands of years of waiting. In the village of Bethlehem, the world's Savior, Jesus, was born. The new Jerusalem is the Church, the assembly of believers in Jesus, the community of worshipers, ourselves. The peace we seek is grounded, therefore, on our relationship with God. When enough persons respond positively to this relationship, the world will be at peace.

Tuesday of the First Week of Advent

Is 11:1-10;
Lk 10:21-24

Today's Gospel is taken from chapter 10 of Luke. In the earlier section, which sets the context of today's reading, the evangelist records the return of the disciples from their preaching assignment. They related their success—even how they had power over Satan—and, perhaps, their failure. At this point, today's Gospel opens with Jesus rejoicing in the Holy Spirit. The cause of his joy is that simple persons, even children, can understand the Good News.

This does not mean that study and learning are obstacles to the Gospel. Sometimes, however, the attitudes generated through higher education could lead some to think that "I know it all," or "I am a cut above the rest of you," or "I have the inside track with God." Degrees may even breed arrogance and presumption. St. Bonaventure, the Franciscan theologian, comforted a weeping woman. She lamented that a simple and uneducated woman could never love God as much as he, the minister general of the Order, cardinal, papal legate, writer and theologian. He reminded the woman of this gospel text and asserted that learning is not the measure of love. Sacrifice and good works are. She, then, could love God more than he.

Simplistic believers prefer religion to be without doctrines, symbols, rituals and creeds. Yet to remain truly *simple*, religion needs all these, lest simplicity become anti-intellectual, sentimental and naive. When religion loses all parameters, *simplicity* becomes a rudderless ship. Simplistic religion paves the way for weak faith and superstition.

Like Bonaventure's weeping woman, religious people do know how to love, whereas the knowledgeable may not know how to be religious. Our faith is able to find the balance: the love of theology and the theology of love.

To use a human expression, God is already very "smart," the font of truth and knowledge. He cannot be influenced or motivated by anything outside himself— least of all by human intellects which he has created. Nevertheless, he surely expects more from those with greater knowledge and better education—which may very well be a burden because of the accountability factor on the day of judgment.

We cannot understand the mystery of God, but we can share in his life. Jesus suggests that the *"childlike"* can easily receive his revelations. The minds of children are filled with wonder. They are readily amazed at the world's marvels. Speed and size impress them; they like to hear stories. Children may more ably penetrate the mysteries of the kingdom than learned adults. Adults, Jesus suggests, need to be open to the Master in trusting faith, which is authentic simplicity.

"No one knows who the Son is except the Father" and vice versa. With such expressions Jesus prepared his Jewish audiences carefully to accept both his divinity and the mystery of the Trinity. The practical application of Jesus' words is our return to the Father from whose creative hand we came. *"No one knows...who the Father is except the Son and anyone to whom the Son wishes to reveal him."* As St. Maximilian Kolbe expressed it, going from the Father at our conception and the individual creation of our souls is the "action" or "flux." Returning to him in heaven is the "reaction or "reflux." The Holy Spirit and his spouse, the Immaculate, are essential agents in this process. The conclusion of many of our prayers reflects this process of coming and going. We pray "in the Holy Spirit through Christ our Lord."

At the Last Supper, Jesus told the apostles that he had disclosed only that which he had heard from the Father. The goal of our spiritual pilgrimage is to reach the Father. Jesus was born into this world to make us adoptive children of the Father, who predestined us all in Christ Jesus. That is why we share in the beatitude of today's Gospel: *"Blessed are the eyes that see what you see."*

Wednesday of the First Week of Advent

Is 25:6-10;
Mt 15:29-37

Usually, the first reading and the Gospel during Advent are not closely coordinated. Today, however, both readings speak of God comforting and healing the ills of the people and then feeding them in an extraordinary way. Isaiah writes, *"The Lord God will wipe away the tears from all faces."* The first paragraph of the Gospel describes the healing of the crippled, deformed, blind and mute. The multiplication of such miracles attracted the large crowd, which led to the dilemma of the second paragraph: how to provide food for so great a number.

The miracle of feeding the thousands was a prediction and foreshadowing of the Eucharist to come. It was so important an event that the story was undoubtedly repeated many times by the faithful until different versions surfaced. Today's reading shows four thousand men and their families being fed, but earlier, in chapter 14, Matthew records five thousand men, not counting women and children. This duplication is called a *doublet,* the technical description for two narrations of the same event. In this case, the *doublet* attests both to the importance of the lesson involved and the prediction of the Eucharist. It also demonstrates that God's revelation is subject to the vicissitudes of human authors. The question always to ask is: "What does the sacred author wish to assert under God's inspiration?"

We read that the large crowd was with Jesus for three days in a relatively deserted area. The food supply was scarce and no doubt individual families had consumed what they had brought. Jesus was moved to pity. Mothers were worried about their children. Youngsters were restless and cranky. The men felt obliged to provide for their families. Jesus often set his wonders and teachings within the crises of daily human events: a groom's embarrassment at Cana; the death of the only son of a widowed mother; an adulteress being stoned for her sin; fretful and hungry families in an isolated location.

Nevertheless, seven loaves and a few fish generated enough leftovers to fill seven hampers. Some scholars downplay this scene and claim that there was no miracle, only charitable sharing inspired by the example of

Jesus and his disciples. However, tradition has always seen this event as a genuine miracle of Jesus.

Another dimension to this miracle surfaces. Several times in the Gospels Jesus "previews," or conversely gives a flashback, of the institution of the Eucharist at the Last Supper. Here, too, he *"gave thanks"* (or blessed God), *"broke"* and distributed the food to his disciples. On Easter he joined Cleophas and Simeon at Emmaus, where "they recognized him in the breaking of the bread" (cf. Lk 24:35).

The Eucharist is the focus of our principal encounter with Christ and sums up the redemption. The Eucharist comes to exist as the fruit of the crucifixion, which is the *instant replay* of Calvary. The crucifixion is repeatedly made present over and over again, no longer to win salvation but to apply salvation concretely and individually throughout human history. The reception of Holy Communion enables the *saved* person to encounter Jesus precisely as his or her Savior. As individuals, we may be sinful and weak, yet God looks upon the faith of his Church which is the body of the perfect, divine and human Christ. We do not elect Jesus as head of the board of directors; he chooses us. Christ not only lives independently, but also in us and through us by his choice. Because we are united with each other by sharing the life of the soul, which is the Holy Spirit, because each of us can name the Father as our own Father, the whole body of Christ is greater than the sum of the members. The Church is eminently the organism where the whole exceeds the sum of its parts.

There are a few lessons to be taken from this narrative. Jesus continues to be moved with pity for the needy, but he still asks his disciples to be intermediaries in feeding the crowds with his word and sacrament. Pray today for religious vocations and encourage the young to follow Jesus with a radical commitment. Of course, we all have our vocation and need to be sensitive to our call to serve the Church and the world. Further, as surrogates of Jesus and stewards of the mysteries of God, we ought to be recognizable in the way we break bread, that is, the way we attend Mass, receive Communion, participate in liturgy, respect the house of God and adore him in the Blessed Sacrament.

On the level of social action, this miracle invites us to continue the multiplication of resources for the poor and to give them access, as is their human right, in Isaiah's poetry, to a *"feast of rich food and choice wines."*

Thursday of the
First Week of Advent

Is 26:1-6;
Mt 7:21, 24-27

Isaiah promises that God will level the cities of the unjust nations, but will keep his holy city strong with walls and ramparts. Our security is to be based on our trust in God.

In today's Gospel, we have the end of Jesus' great sermon on the mount. This is at least a dozen sermons from Jesus' public life. The disciples remembered and perhaps jotted them down. Later Matthew collected them. Rather than place each separate speech where it had been spoken, he strings these sayings of Jesus together into one long garland. The sermon includes the beatitudes, the Our Father, the nature of discipleship, the Jewish law, various sins and virtues, prayer, riches, the golden rule of Christ and, finally, today's text.

The opening paragraph warns against hypocrisy, that is, praying loudly and visibly, while not doing God's will. In verses 22 and 23 which have not been included in today's text, even the false prophets, exorcists and miracle workers get their deserved rebuke from Jesus. When they present themselves at the gates of heaven claiming, "Look at all we did in your name," the answer will be direct: "Out of my sight, you evildoers!" Jesus' point is that sometimes apparently dedicated, zealous individuals, even priests and religious, could act independently of the Father's will.

No doubt we have all been guilty of such ego trips occasionally. Instead, responding to the will of God requires humility, submission and cooperation. In other words, what good is it to give God one thing when he is asking for something else? It must be God who assigns the spectacular tasks in his Church. We are not to choose "grandstand plays." Imagine how God would judge you if you died today: not by those rare camera-ready displays, but by the consistent pattern of your daily actions, doing the right thing without fanfare.

Jesus concludes by telling us to build our spiritual houses on the rock of humility, not on the shifting sands of elusive popularity and shallow piety. When winds and rains begin to buffet the house, that is, problems and difficulties such as the roof caving in, the sump giving out, the foundations eroding and the electric power failing, we had better be embedded in the rock of Christ.

Jesus must have had the typical Palestinian terrain in mind and it may have been during the winter rains. Limestone terraces formed from centuries of erosion of the mountainsides are common throughout the Holy Land. People build houses on the terraces, cementing their dwellings into the limestone itself. Whatever is not well anchored to the rocky cliffs may wash down the steep mountainsides. The limestone terraces also support olive groves, vineyards and orchards. Sand and gravel, which is unstable during heavy rains, accumulates along the base of the mountains and hills. A stream, swelling with rain water, may easily wash away the houses.

The Advent lesson is clear. We cannot prevent or eliminate anxieties and can barely avoid sin, but if we try to understand God's will for us, we are shoring up the foundations of our spiritual house on the rock which is Jesus Christ himself.

Friday of the
First Week of Advent

Is 29:17-24;
Mt 9:27-31

The Gospel text that immediately precedes today's text reads, "News of this circulated through the district." News of what? That a child had been raised from the dead. Therefore, others were attracted to the Lord, searching for help in their infirmity and relief from pain. Two blind men, thinking that restoration of eyesight was much less than the restoration of life, sought out Jesus, the Son of David.

Scholars tell us this cure is a *doublet* or repetition of the same cure in chapter 20, because the blind man in that episode also calls Jesus Son of David. This is a reminder of God's promise to King David centuries earlier: that his offspring would always rule the Chosen People. In Jesus' time, when David's line seemed to have disappeared, the return of a Son of David would also signal the appearance of the Messiah. Yet this title probably did not please Jesus at the time. He refused the role of a political leader and the would-be liberator from Roman rule. Thus he *"sternly"* warned the cured men not to tell anyone.

A second reason for Jesus telling the two blind men not to publicize their cure is more deeply spiritual. Although his compassion led him to cure the disabled, he preached fundamentally to cure souls and offer spiritual healing. He wished the people to hear his spiritual message concerning the kingdom, not to be awestruck by wonders and miracles.

People sought the sensational. They were attracted to the visionary, the miracle-worker, the prophet, the exorcist. Perhaps their faith was weak and required such buttressing. Nevertheless, the Advent lesson for us is to seek God in the ordinary, typical and human, not the extraordinary and superhuman.

Have you heard the expression (which was also a television commercial), "Reach out and touch someone"? Several times this expression is lived out by Jesus in the gospels through: the children he embraced, the spittle-and-mud plaster he applied to the eyes and ears of a handicapped person, the handclasps of friendship. This was the touch of the Master's hand.

Remember the child who was scared at night? His mother comforted the little one in bed with: "Don't worry, God is with you." During Advent we remember that God is made manifest in Jesus. He is God in human flesh, which is what the frightened child wanted.

We like to shake hands. We like to hug and kiss, to fondle babies, to get a backrub, simply to be held when we are in grief. The touch of "skin on skin" can be degrading and sinful, or it can be elevating and chaste, uplifting and affirming. We recall at this time of the year that Jesus became incarnate to sanctify our human activities. So "reach out" today and "touch someone's" life. Best of all, touch someone with whom you want to spend eternity. Then someone "blind" may suddenly see.

Miracles are not a denial of the laws of nature. They are merely the affirmation that the Author of nature is able to make exceptions or suspend the laws he embedded in the universe. A miracle is never spontaneous or "lucky" or an accident. A miracle is part of God's plan. The best way miracles can happen to us is to let ourselves become part of God's plan and to ready ourselves through prayer for the touch of his hand.

Saturday of the First Week of Advent

Is 30:19-21, 23-26;
Mt 9:35—10:1, 6-8

Bread, water, grain and cattle—these are rather earthbound symbols of plenty and do not sound very spiritual, but we must read the Jewish Testament in the light of its fulfillment in the Christian dispensation of grace. The Church seems to take this view in linking today's two readings. Isaiah wrote, *"He will give rain for the seed that you sow in the ground. And the wheat that the soil produces will be rich and abundant."* In Matthew 9, Jesus tells his disciples, *"The harvest is abundant but the laborers are few; so ask the master of the harvest to send out laborers for his harvest."* Jesus spiritualizes what is earthbound. He compares the grain bending and shimmering in the wind to people's souls. The Father, master of the harvest, will provide the vocations to bring in the sheaves.

It is helpful when reading the Bible, especially the Old Testament, to see this collection of books not only as God's revelation to mankind, but also as mankind's response to that revelation. This includes some responses that we are to avoid, such as idolatry, adultery and lying. God chooses the events of world history to create salvation history for the family of God in its development.

One fact emerges with great clarity: God's plan forges ahead with inevitability. It cannot be reversed. We can only speed it up or slow it down to some degree by virtue or vice. When the Bible identifies God as the "Totally Other," the implication refers to our human transitoriness. We do not have to be; we do not have to exist. And if we do not make it into the kingdom of God, then our existence was pointless. Our life was irrelevant. Although we do not condemn Judas, we remember that Jesus said it would have been better if Judas had not been born. God, on the other hand, must exist for the world to have any meaning. The Bible encapsulates the relationships between the living, true, eternal God and transitory human beings. Therefore, we can learn from the Bible what man is and what he is destined to become under God.

In the Bible, God enters human history to bring it to its destined close. He expects us to lift up stakes, turn ourselves around, take a less-traveled road, hitch our wagon to a star we cannot even see—simply at his word. Then he can also take his time in using us. This is our purification-time, the desert experience, cliff-hanging by our fingernails.

Jesus told the disciples to *"Go rather to the lost sheep of the house of Israel."* Today's reading omits verse 5: "Do not visit pagan territory and do not enter a Samaritan town." It appears that Jesus did not want his disciples to lose credibility with the Jews by becoming ritually impure by contact with non-Jews, their customs and food. The fact that Jesus was known for not observing Pharisaic restrictions proved problem enough for his movement. Further, Jesus was sent first of all to the Jews, then only to the Gentiles. He told this to the woman from Tyre who wanted only to eat the crumbs of the banquet Jesus was setting before the Jews (cf. Mt 15:26).

The people were exhausted from following Jesus, today's Gospel reads. They had to lie down like sheep without a shepherd. Cattle can be left in the field unattended, but sheep need supervision. They must be taken out in the morning and returned to the fold at night. They are easily spooked by strangers. They wander off if no one familiar calls to them. Their wool gets tangled in briars and they fall into ditches. Sheep are easy prey to wild beasts and thieves. They don't even seek shade in the burning sun.

It is fairly easy to apply this physical metaphor to our human experiences and our need for the Good Shepherd. The teaching of Jesus and our proper response can be learned by studying the Bible daily, so we can become part of salvation history and God's plan.

Solemnity of the Immaculate Conception

Gn 3:9-15, 20;
Eph 1:3-6, 11-12;
Lk 1:26-38

Today we have the overlapping of mysteries. Every celebration of Mary includes her Son and vice versa. The feast of one suggests the role of the other. Mary's Immaculate Conception in the womb of her mother occurred through the foreseen redemption by Jesus on the cross, for Mary, too, was a child of Adam, subject to original sin according to nature, but without sin of any kind according to grace. We must remember that, although Jesus was conceived miraculously in Mary's womb by the power of the Holy Spirit, Mary herself was conceived in the normal human way through the agency of her natural parents. Thus today's Gospel may be a little misleading. The Gospel of the Annunciation refers to Jesus' earthly beginning, but the solemnity of the Immaculate Conception refers to Mary's earthly beginning. The spiritual message of Luke's text, of course, refers simply to the holiness of Mary whom God used in salvation history.

No reporter with a tape recorder or video camera was present for the dialogues recounted in Genesis and Luke, so we must ask scholars for the theological meaning of the two conversations and the parallel ideas: Adam and Christ, Eve and Mary, serpent and angel, defeat and victory, fall and rising, loss and gain, death and life. What did Adam and Eve lose? They lost their elevated nature which consisted of: gifts of knowledge, sanctifying grace, freedom from want and suffering, the ability not to die, the proper relationship between mankind and God, between each other and nature. We have recovered some of this, but still struggle to regain the rest, particularly the relationships.

The healing of relationships began with the new creation, the New Covenant, the New Testament, the new Eve and Adam. The Fathers of the Church called Mary the dawn and Jesus the rising sun. Just as the dawn comes before sunrise, so Mary precedes Jesus in the order of time. The dawn does not cause the sun. The sun causes the dawn. Thus Jesus is the reason for Mary's special role, graces and prerogatives. That is why Jesus is Mary's savior as well as ours. Jesus did not allow her to be subject to sin because he was going to take his flesh, his human nature, from her person. We find a suggestion of all this in the second reading from Ephesians: *"He* (God) *chose us* (Mary, too) *in him* (Christ), *before the foundation of the world, to be holy and without blemish before him. In love he destined us for adoption to himself through Jesus Christ.... In him* (Christ) *we* (especially Mary) *were also chosen, destined in accord with the purpose of the One who accomplishes all things according to the intention of his will, so that we might exist for the praise of his glory, we who first hoped in Christ."* Obviously, at the Annunciation, Mary was the first to hope in Christ and praise God. She was truly the one *"in love"* which is another way of proclaiming her sinlessness.

Mary's singular graces sometimes seem to make her too distant and intangible. She did not even merit her special form of redemption because she had not yet been born. However, as the Franciscan theologian, Duns

Scotus, wrote, "God was able to do this; it was fitting that he act so; therefore, he actually did it."

St. Maximilian Kolbe said that Mary's Immaculate Conception was the reason for her becoming the Mother of God. It is her principal title, one that she gave herself at Lourdes. Actually, theologians consistently point out that her singular holiness is more significant than her very motherhood. This is based on a particular scene in the Gospel and the words of her Son. When the woman in the crowd called out to Jesus, "Blessed is the womb that bore you and the breasts that nourished you," the Lord answered, "Rather blessed are they who hear the word of God and keep it" (cf. Lk 11:27-28). In her singular holiness, Mary became the keeper of the word, the rememberer, the ponderer, as she is considered in chapter 2 of Luke. St. Augustine explained that Mary first conceived Jesus in her heart and mind—spiritually— before conceiving him physically. She stands for the nourishing Church. St. Ambrose wrote that everything said of Mary may also be ascribed to the Church and everything said of the Church may also be attributed to Mary.

Mary consented to live an atypical life with faith alone as guide and dependent on the Father's providence. She was only a teenager when she took on the responsibilities of motherhood coupled with the restrictions of virginity. When she called herself the *"handmaid"* of the Lord, she manifested herself in the classic biblical sense as a poor nobody, who lacks clout and resources for the future. Yet she could cry out, "My soul magnifies the Lord and my spirit rejoices in God my Savior."

We cannot be excessive in our praise of the one whom God himself chose to honor so much. Remember, no one ever has God fully for Father until he has Mary for mother. To be like Jesus means precisely that.

SECOND WEEK
OF ADVENT

Second Sunday
of Advent, A

Is 11:1-10; Rom 15:4-9
Mt 3:1-12

The text from Isaiah is among the most often quoted lines of the Jewish Testament. You will hear it from the pulpit and read it on Christmas cards. Wolves, lions and bears will hobnob with their natural prey, lambs and goats. Babies, always curious and getting into things, will poke their hands into the dens of venomous snakes. These figures of speech make a mighty metaphor of a return to paradise, where nature and mankind lived in harmony.

The playful child is, of course, a subtle reference to Baby Jesus. And what a Child he is. What a man he will become. The seven gifts of the Holy Spirit (called simply the *"spirit of the LORD"* in the Jewish Testament, because the Trinity had not yet been revealed) are described. These gifts, more fully explained in Catholic theology about the Third Person of the Trinity, are qualities of the coming Messiah, foreseen by Isaiah. This Messiah will belong to the house and family of David, whose father was Jesse. So the text begins, *"A shoot shall sprout from the stump of Jesse."* The ideas of Isaiah are echoed in Romans today. Paul points out that what had been written (in the Jewish Testament) *"was written for our instruction."* He asks God to enable the Romans *"to think in harmony with one another,"* as Isaiah prophesied for the messianic reign. Isaiah wrote, *"The root of Jesse...the Gentiles shall seek out."* Paul said, *"...so that the Gentiles might glorify God for his mercy."* The point is that we have to know Jesus to understand the scriptures that precede him. Through these pages, the Lord who is Christ slowly takes form, develops stature and achieves visibility so we can believe in the true God and true man.

We all love parties, but we can get carried away, even for our Christian party, Christmas. Thanksgiving Friday is the biggest shopping spree of the nation and shopkeepers report their sales on national television. Yet the day after Christmas the faded and shopworn decorations are ready for burning or resale. Our money is as used up as our holiday spirit and our charity because taxes will soon be due. In some parts of the country, "white Christmas" leads inevitably to a gray and slushy New Year.

Nevertheless, you can remain in joy and retain the Christmas spirit long after the holiday if you have kept Advent faithfully in an attitude of repentance and a posture of supplication. Christian spirituality requires waiting for God's visitation. This is one dimension of the so-called "desert experience," recalling the wandering of the Jews during the Exodus. The prophets, the last of whom was John the Baptist, relished the spiritual uplift that came from dependence in isolation upon God for sustenance, direction and purpose. When the Jews settled down and settled into cities with no miraculous manna nor water from the rock, they also no longer experienced the awe and wonder at the mighty works of the Lord.

John the Baptist was the voice crying from the desert, his ground of experience and vantage point of spiritual success. In this he is the model of all preachers. We can prepare the Lord's way only in John's way, through prayer and sacrifice. As cousins, John and Jesus may have been bearded look-alikes; their ministry made them act-alikes. Both were harassed for the truth they proclaimed and finally were murdered.

When John saw the hypocritical scribes and Pharisees coming into the Jordan River for his baptism of repentance (Jesus had not yet proclaimed the baptism of new life), he told them to give some evidence *"of your repentance."* The same words could apply to us.

Striking parallels emerge from the stories of the two cousins, John and Jesus. Both births were announced by an angel. Elizabeth was beyond the age of child-bearing; Mary conceived miraculously. The canticles of both Zechariah and Mary, poetic and prophetic, are ascribed to the two events. Neighbors marveled at what John would become; the shepherds and Magi who visited Jesus were similarly struck. John came out of the desert, perhaps Qumran, to begin his ministry. Jesus began his ministry by forty days of fasting in the mountain wilderness. Their themes were repentance and conversion. The scribes and Pharisees, as in today's Gospel, were chastised by John and Jesus and King Herod sought the life of both.

Jesus, however, as our supreme model, lived a life more able to be imitated. He did not dine on locusts and honey, wear odd garments and sweat in the desert heat. He lived like other Jews in a Palestinian village. Thus Jesus diverts our gaze from sensationalism and extreme penance to sober moderation and attainable spiritual goals.

After we have finished wondering about the astonishing career of John the Baptist, the bottom line of today's teaching is that God looks for a change of heart in us, not grandstand plays. This is what John told the

Pharisees and I am sure some were honest in their conversion, so for them John's baptism was more than their just getting on the bandwagon. We, too, must alter our thinking and make up for past prejudices, unkindnesses, put-downs, ethnic or racial slurs, exploitation of the helpless, manipulation of others and intolerance. John said of Jesus, *"His winnowing fan is in his hand. He will clear his threshing floor and gather his wheat into his barn, but the chaff he will burn with unquenchable fire."*

Second Sunday
of Advent, B

Is 40:1-5, 9-11;
2 Pt 3:8-14; Mk 1:1-8

The second and third Sundays of all three Advent cycles center on the mission of St. John the Baptist. This reflects the broader vision of the Church going beyond the coming of Jesus at Christmas. Last Sunday focused on his coming at the end of the world. Today, Mark's Gospel introduces Jesus' coming into his public life.

The first reading from Isaiah suggests hope, but without the threats of earlier Isaian texts. Jerusalem has already been destroyed, the people are captives and their sins have been paid twice over. But the Holy City will be restored and *"the glory of the LORD shall be revealed."* This is an allusion to the sanctuary of the Temple, where the *shekinah*, the "glory of God," manifests itself. The author completely bypasses the royal house of David (because they had lost the wars, given in to idolatry and over-taxed the citizens) and proclaims that the Lord God will be king.

Whenever a king traveled, the local people prepared for his visit in several ways: by storing up provisions for his entourage, by providing a suitable dwelling and by repairing the local roads so the royal carriage or chariot might not bounce over the potholes and get stuck in the ruts. Thus both Isaiah and John the Baptist in today's Gospel call out like the old-time town crier, "Hear ye, hear ye! The king is coming soon!" John actually repeats Isaiah, *"In the desert prepare the way of the LORD! Make straight in the wasteland a highway for our God! Every valley shall be filled in, every mountain and hill shall be laid low; The rugged land shall be made a plain, the rough country a broad valley."*

"Prepare the way of the LORD." Perhaps *"way"* should be capitalized in memory of him who called himself the Way, Truth and Life. In the Acts of the Apostles, the first disciples were called followers of *"the Way"* (Acts 9:2). *"Make straight"* means to avoid the detours of sin and the dangerous curves of temptation. So bring low the mountains of self-sufficiency and fill the valleys of emptiness with virtue and prayer. The rough and rugged terrain of uncharitableness should be smoothed out with kindness, generosity and thoughtfulness.

This forerunner of Jesus, his cousin, John the Baptist, was not a man of compromise, not soft-spoken. He told it "like it is." Each of the four evangelists are known by a symbol. Mark's symbol is a lion because he starts his Gospel with John the Baptist, who sounded like a lion roaring in the desert. (There were lions still roaming around the Judean desert in ancient days.) Because John was a consecrated Nazirite, like Samson and some other prophets, he no doubt looked like a shaggy lion, feisty and weatherbeaten. In 2 Kings 1:8, Elijah the Tishbite is described as *"wearing a hairy garment with a leather girdle about his loins."* Elijah was even more aggressive than John. The Bible refers to John as Elijah-returned-to-earth.

So John was bare-chested, thin, wearing a camel's hair cloak which doubled as his scratchy blanket and a kind of kilt or Bermuda shorts made of leather—very handy to run around a desert filled with thorns and bushes. His diet was high in protein and sugar, but would never become a "blue-plate special" unless preceded by several martinis.

Neither Mark nor I are recommending John's lifestyle, but rather his admonitions: to straighten out our lives and make way for the Lord; to repent and get the "desert experience" where we will be alone with God in our personal *poustinia*, a "wasteland." I tried this experience at the Franciscan *poustinia* outside of El Qubeibeh, about twelve miles outside of Jerusalem. I was alone with God, on the spur of a mountain surrounded by a stone wall. I had a small hut with a large plain cross, a thermos of water and some bread. Some repeat the "Jesus Prayer" endlessly and wait for God's visitation. I recited decades of the Rosary instead. (This experience has been described by the late Baroness Catherine de Hueck Doherty.)

Actually we often "romanticize" asceticism, overstate the attraction of monastic life and fantasize about the joys of seclusion. Even the poustinia is rather contrived and available to only a few. Fundamental Christian asceticism is derived from the trials and upsets of daily life and personal relationships. And when a Christian ascetic "gives up" some indulgence, it is not because cigarettes, television, sex, liquor and movies are intrinsically evil (only extrinsically when they are sins), but rather the ascetic is choosing something better: freedom from distractions and temptations, time for meditation and prayer, service to the Church and world.

Those who enter the way of suffering or privation must beware of imposing it on others, be careful they don't talk too much about it and be sure they are not motivated by a low self-esteem. It is better, nevertheless, to be a "closet" sufferer than to play to the grandstand. St. Paul did glory in his cross (cf. Gal 6:14) but Jesus prayed, "Let this chalice pass from me" (Lk 22:42). He submitted to his Father's will—which is the bottom line of Christian ascetics—and was never so successful as when he seemed a failure on the cross. As you straighten out your road for God's entry into your life and fill in the pot holes, remember that unforeseen suffering (our personal *poustinia*) is sometimes the only crack in our self-protective armor that allows God to penetrate and take possession of us.

Second Sunday of Advent, C

Bar 5:1-9;
Phil 1:4-6, 8-11; Lk 3:1-6

The first reading is ascribed to Baruch, the secretary of Jeremiah the prophet. Even though his authorship is not certain, we believe, nevertheless, that this text is inspired. Baruch comforts Israel with a poem. Part of the nation has returned from captivity, but still no Temple has been rebuilt to serve as a rallying point for the Jewish people. To encourage Israel, Baruch calls the Holy City their mother and queen. God will flatten the mountains—perhaps an allusion to idolatrous worship in the high places—and plant shade trees along the hot, dusty roads of Israel. The spiritual application is, of course, that God smashes down sin and shelters us under his power.

In his letter to his parishioners at Philippi, Paul continues this theme: *"...the one who began a good work in you will continue to complete it until the day of Christ Jesus."* *"Day"* refers to the Second Coming, the final judgment.

John the Baptist's preaching is like *deja vu*, a repeat of the situation of the time of Baruch. Jerusalem is again in captivity. In chapter 3 of his Gospel, Luke points out that Palestine is divided by the various rulers he names. Annas, head of the high-priestly family, kept the office in the family by getting his son-in-law, Caiaphas, ap-

pointed. The latter was official high priest at the crucifixion of Jesus. Meanwhile, in Rome the half-crazy
Sejanus ruled, while Emperor Tiberius retired to Capri
(an island off the coast of Naples) and lived in sexual
excesses that were the scandal of an ancient world not
noted for its chastity.

How similar those times are to our own. The world
today is divided between the strongest powers, who vie
for world control. Political scandals, stock market thiev-
ery, abortion and pornography remind us that times
don't change. We need to hear again the thundering
phrase of John the Baptist: Repentance leads to the forgiveness of our sins.

The spiritual life is not destroyed by falling down-
ward into sin, but by staying down without repentance.
Sin is reparable; despair is the language of hell. We don't
have to act like supermen and superwomen to be saints.
After a while we can graciously accept even our weak-
nesses and limitations, such as poor health and a slow
mind, because our expectations become realistic and our
self-concept more honest. Holiness is built on honest
insights about our crosses.

On the long walk of life, it is better to have a well
worn pair of shoes. Thus familiar and accustomed
crosses tend to fit us better, unless God suddenly leaves
us comfortably barefoot. Crosses generally keep us honest. Honesty leads to repentance and repentance up-
roots sin. Today's liturgy points out that the eradication
of sin is the first step to holiness. We await Christmas
with the words of the Baptist in our ears.

We note that Christmas is not even mentioned ob-
liquely in the readings today. Instead, John comes out of
the desert across the Jordan as a reminder to Israel that
a holy nation was forged in the desert of Sinai. There
God met his people in a holy covenant. He agreed to
cherish the Jews forever, as the apple of his eye (cf. Ps

17:8). With all the manifestations of God in sacred history, Christmas is very meaningful and we should understand that covenant, too.

No doubt you are in the midst of writing Christmas mail, perhaps while listening to carols over the radio. It is easy to deduce that Christmas is becoming too commercialized. We don't really give gifts freely, from the heart. Rather, we exchange gifts, comparing the probable prices. We will soon have to rush out to get cards for those whom we overlooked, but who sent a card to us. Not just the "good" children get gifts, but often the most unruly and spoiled as well. Poor Saint Nicholas, the bishop from southern Italy. He has been turned into Santa Claus, who moved to the North Pole, married Mrs. Claus and lives year-round with pixies and elves until he can get away on December 24. Now he is the patron saint of department stores!

How far from the poor, cold, crying Babe of Bethlehem. Look, the Advent season is still here, so you have time to find your personal desert in which to pray and prepare for an encounter with God. Don't give a gift so that you will receive one, but rather because God has given you his gifts. Don't worry about how many shopping days until Christmas, but how many praying days.

Monday of the Second Week of Advent

Is 35:1-10;
Lk 5:17-26

We have already seen how Jesus wanted to call attention to his message rather than to his sensational healing powers. In today's Gospel, Jesus cured the paralytic physically as the sign of his spiritual healing. Jesus even clarified his motives to the scribes and Pharisees: *"But that you may know that the Son of Man has authority on earth to forgive sins."*

The fame of this new rabbi, Jesus, attracted observers and hostile critics from all over Palestine, especially the experts in Jewish laws and customs. We can surmise that they may have seen a rival in Jesus who might reduce their own popularity or win over their students. Itinerant rabbis were not unusual in those days. They "lived off the land," so to speak, by handouts and gifts from benefactors and the beneficiaries of their ministry.

The rabbis of the Holy Land liked to be surrounded by a group of admiring students as a testimony of their effectiveness as teachers. It is always unfortunate and debasing when a public figure requires adulation and applause and when his or her ego depends on the affirmation of others. On the other hand, Jesus' disciples were such a motley crew, such an unsophisticated lot, that their adherence to the Master, who in any case was abrasive at times and even inflammatory, actually threatened no one's popularity.

The text does not make it clear how a full-grown man on a mat could be lowered through the roof of a house. There were two possibilities. Some houses had roof tiles and slats which could be removed so that the cot could be slowly lowered by ropes. Other houses had outside staircases from the courtyard or street to the roof with a trapdoor giving access to the rooms below. Once the man was inside the crowded house, his infirmity was healed and his sins were forgiven.

The enemies of Jesus made an important theological statement, perhaps unwittingly playing into Jesus' plan, when they posed their critical question, *"Who but God alone can forgive sins?"* Contemporary Jews would have been shocked and outraged if Jesus had proclaimed bluntly, "I am God's Son, equal to him. In fact, I am God!" So he performed the works of God, such as the forgiveness of sins in today's text. At other times, he acted as the Lord of the Sabbath (cf. Mt 12:8), announced that he would return for judgment on the final Day of the Lord and stated such ideas as, *"The Father and I are one"* (Jn 10:30) and *"Whoever has seen me has seen the Father"* (Jn 14:9).

The readings of today not only prepare us for understanding the humanity of the Word of God in the Nativity, but they remind us through today's Gospel that Jesus Christ is divine as well. The Creed sums it up as Light from Light and true God from true God. Yet that Word was made flesh and made his dwelling among us. Like the bystanders in today's Gospel who were seized with astonishment, let us also give praise to God.

Tuesday of the
Second Week of Advent

Is 40:1-11;
Mt 18:12-14

Chapter 18 is the "children's" hour in Matthew's Gospel. It begins with Jesus' admonition to his disciples to change and become like little children. Next the chapter warns that anyone who scandalizes a child should be thrown into the sea with a millstone around his neck—a sure guarantee of drowning. In Matthew 18:10, Jesus says that the guardian angels of children constantly behold his heavenly Father's face. He continues then with the example of the lost sheep—just one out of one hundred— who is a stray, maybe even a maverick. Jesus' final warning is that God does not want a single sheep to be lost, just as a parent would not want his or her child to be lost in a shopping mall.

Jesus often makes statements that upset us and there is just such a statement today: the Good Shepherd is happier about finding the maverick than in having ninety-nine dependable sheep who did not wander off into trouble. In terms of numbers and fidelity, the ninety-nine seem to be more important. Of course, we may assume that their ultimate reward will be the greater for their dependability. But the Lord is merely trying to tell us that every individual is important. Attempting to save the erring members of a flock may require taking risks with the major or larger part of a congregation or parish.

The paradox is that God needs nothing, but wants everything from us for two reasons: Our surrender to him is an acknowledgement that everything good came from him in the first place. Secondly, he wants to return to us our everything, blessed and purified. It may be difficult to realize that each of us matters to God. He did not start the human race to enslave us, but to give us freedom. We may misuse that freedom to wander and get lost, but there is so much joy in being found.

It often seems that the traditional members of a parish do not want the pastor to delve too deeply into peace and social justice movements, nor to raise some sensitive political or moral issues. Yet a priest, as the dispenser of God's graces, is obliged to stand back, review and judge the world and its values.

Even though chapter 18 refers principally to children, Jesus used the term "little ones." This may be applied to the ordinary, down-to-earth believer. He or she has to work hard for a living, tries to figure out God's will and frequently falls into sin. This is what most of us are: "little ones." Nevertheless, the Good Shepherd considers us important and will inevitably come after us when we fall into a culvert, get scratched in the briars, or hide in a cave until the wolves pass by.

The Incarnation means this: The strays are getting rounded up, the flock is growing, the word is going out to the little ones—to us, the sinners. The mercy of God is available to all. As sometimes foolish sheep, even though we walk in the valley of the shadow of death, we fear no evil, because his rod and his staff steady and comfort us (cf. Ps 23:4).

Wednesday of the
Second Week of Advent

Is 40:25-31;
Mt 11:28-30

Perhaps you began Advent a week and a half ago with the promises that you would attend Mass and receive Communion or recite the Rosary for a special intention every day. You could be growing impatient because God is so slow to answer your prayers and your trust is getting a little shaky. Ten days ago you may have thought that your prayers were reparation enough for weeks and months of neglect, indifference and even sin. Today the Gospel provides a heartening text from Matthew.

Do you ever get weary and find just existing and surviving to be a great weight on your soul? Sometimes in the morning, do you just hate to put your foot out of bed onto the cold floor? Does your week have seven "blue Mondays" and you wish it were Friday on Tuesdays? Do things change so fast that you can't keep up? Like Alice in Wonderland, do you run as fast as you can just to stay in the same place? If so, then Jesus is talking to you.

"I will give you rest," he says. Everyone's idea of rest and refreshment is different according to one's experiences: a cool breeze when the air conditioner is down, a cold drink on a hot August afternoon, sleeping late and ignoring the alarm clock on a cold winter day, driving around a turn in the highway into full view of beautiful mountains, lingering in an art gallery with your favorite pictures. Although Jesus would not exclude these human refreshments, in today's Gospel he is speaking of spiritual refreshment. Jesus sends an uplifting thought

and an encouraging word when we are depressed. He sends a friend when someone puts us down or when we fail at an important task. He inspires us with the hope of "heaven-to-come" when we are burdened with sin.

God's answer to our prayer, like that of most earthly parents, is often simply, "no." But he does not leave us orphans, bereft of comfort. If we are not comforted by our religious values and insights, we have to search our own hearts. Perhaps through our own neglect and indifference we have lost our taste for spiritual food and refreshment.

The clue to refreshment and consolation is found in the entire text: *"Take my yoke upon you and learn of me."* The scribes and Pharisees often referred to the collection of the many Jewish laws as "the yoke," like the one worn by a beast of burden. Jesus did not do away with the law, but merely says his yoke is easy and his burden light. He, too, requires submission to his law of love and his justice, tempered by mercy. Instead of the complex Jewish system of obligations, Jesus asks us to learn from his own meek and humble heart.

In the present competitive world, Jesus remains a beacon of sanity by proposing gentleness and humility to replace the world's aggression, manipulation and coercion. Put on the Lord's yoke of love today. Imitate his humility and learn patience with others—but with yourself most of all.

Thursday of the
Second Week of Advent

Is 41:13-20;
Mt 11:11-15

The Gospel today records the closing verses of Jesus' final comments about his cousin, John the Baptist, made during Jesus' dialogue with John's followers. Meanwhile, John had been jailed for criticizing Herod's royal family. John knew that he would be executed in prison, so he wanted to transfer his disciples to Jesus. Yet he was still asking for some final confirmation of Jesus' mission.

Jesus answered the queries of the Baptist's disciples by affirming John's mission and praising him as the greatest person in history prior to that moment. Yet Jesus stated that the least important of his own disciples was superior even to John. So John is made out to be greater than Moses, David, Solomon and the prophets and patriarchs. Yet the least believer in Jesus and possessor of grace exceeds the Baptist in spiritual effectiveness and participation in the revealed mysteries of the Father's kingdom. This was not to claim that we are holier than John, more pleasing to God, or more significant in salvation history and in the Church than the forerunner of Christ. Jesus simply meant that we are more knowledgeable about salvation and can achieve a deeper intimacy with the Lord because we have received the fullness of the Good News. Implicit in this dialogue with the Baptist's followers is that Jesus himself must be the greatest in the New Testament and superior to John.

"The kingdom of heaven suffers violence." The religious leaders opposed John despite (or perhaps because of) his asceticism and uncompromising boldness. At that moment in history, Jesus was also being opposed, although he was not such an extreme ascetic. Jesus is telling us that hostility to the Gospel is normal or at least typical. To overcome this bitter opposition, the followers of Christ must take the kingdom of God by storm and by violence. Yet—paradoxically—the warfare must be chiefly against oneself.

It is necessary to set each remark of Jesus into the context of the total message. Elsewhere he is clear that meekness, gentleness and humility of heart are the qualities and virtues he prizes in opposition to violence and aggression (cf. Mt 11:29).

Earlier in this chapter of Matthew, Jesus was asked whether he was *"the one who is to come."* This is a reference to Elijah who, it is said, went to heaven without passing through the gates of death (cf. 2 Kgs 2). On the contrary, says the Lord, John is really more like Elijah in his violent responses to the evil King Herod and to the corruption of his contemporaries. Therefore if John's followers were ready to understand John's mission as the return of Elijah to this earth to die (as was supposed to happen before the final messianic age), then they should be ready to accept Jesus precisely as the true Messiah. Meanwhile John was fulfilling the prophecies about the qualities of the Messiah, especially that the poor would have the Gospel preached to them (cf. Mt 11:5).

Friday of the Second Week of Advent

Is 48:17-19; Mt 11:16-19

Jesus is characteristically gentle to repentant sinners and to simple, but confused hearers. Yet he knows how to be stern with the intransigent. Imagine the scene. Some children were playing nearby or in the next street, oblivious and indifferent to the adults around Jesus. Perhaps these were the children of Jesus' hearers. They may have been bored by the preaching and wandered away to play, or their parents may have told them to "go play someplace" while the Master was talking.

Jesus customarily used tangible, proximate examples to illustrate his sermons—lilies of the field, grain ripe for the harvest, the unproductive fig tree, the lost coin. The merriment of the children and their argument over the song and dance routine caught Jesus' attention and he struck a comparison with his adult audience. The children in the scene were apparently "at war" with each other over the games. They were yelling some jingle or ritual in child's chant, which escapes our modern understanding. Children today might sing, "The farmer in the dell," or "Rain, rain, go away."

The point Jesus made was that, no matter what message his audience heard, nothing satisfied them. They wanted to play their own games with God. Some wanted a totally spiritual, otherworldly message. Some wanted to be washed from their sins and baptized in the Jordan. Others wanted a political Messiah to overthrow the Romans. Still others wished to revive the former monarchy, as under David and Solomon, or revive the old theocracy, focused on Temple worship. Controversy always dredges up the highest virtue and the lowest vice.

So Jesus answered as if to say, "You're damned if you do and you're damned if you don't." If you fast like John and appear the ascetic, the people don't like it. Eat what is set before you and you are called a glutton. It is like that children's game.

It is time to pause halfway through Advent and ask, "What do I expect from God? Is he supposed to dance like the children to my tune? Will I change if I get my wish? Is it not better to change first so as to be worthy of my wish? Do I make of my Christian vocation just a game with God, playing hard-to-get?"

Most of all, the message of Jesus is this: Stop acting like a spoiled child, squatting on the curb and bawling because God won't indulge you and play your silly, childish games!

Saturday of the Second Week of Advent

Sir 48:1-4, 9-11;
Mt 17:10-13

The evangelists were not concerned to set the events of Jesus' life in chronological order, but according to themes or topics. This makes the narratives more logical, but at the expense of accurate history. Both the first reading from Sirach and today's Gospel consider Elijah. Matthew records the dialogues as taking place when Jesus and certain disciples were descending Mt. Tabor. On this same mountain, the Transfiguration had taken place, during which Moses and Elijah flanked Jesus in the apparition (cf. Mt 17:1-8).

Elijah was supposed to return to earth before the endtime and the arrival of the Messiah. Sirach apostrophizes Elijah in these words: *"You are destined, it is written, in time to come to put an end to wrath before the day of the LORD."* The supposition is that if John the Baptist were Elijah come back to earth, then Jesus is the Messiah, appearing in the last age of the world.

Elijah is described as being carried off to heaven in a chariot of fire, drawn by flaming horses (cf. 2 Kgs 2). The tradition is that—because all men die—Elijah must return to this human obligation of death before the return of the Messiah at the end of the world. The sequel in Second Kings is quite interesting. Crotchety Elijah leaves his mantle, a symbol of power, to his disciple, Elisha, who is equally feisty (cf. 2 Kgs 2:9-14).

Jesus answered the questions of his disciples by asserting that John the Baptist was, indeed, Elijah returned to earth. The very fact that the four evangelists take great pains to define the Baptist's role and his subordination to Christ shows John's significance even after his death. The gospels stress the need to understand the transitoriness of John in salvation history. Yet their destinies are linked: both John and Jesus were recognized as prophets, persecuted and killed.

It seems that a prophet is always destined to be a thorn in the side of others. In our day we often hear the title of prophet attributed to psychologists, social scientists and even politicians. This may be the connotation, but the precise denotation is "mouthpiece," that is, God's spokesperson. Yet if the message is not spiritual and correct theologically, the attribution is fallacious. It is anomalous that the world criticizes the Church for being "worldly," that is, most like itself. Yet even such statements by a world that is passing away may be prophetic (cf. 1 Jn 2:17). But it is safer to trust our critics within the Church, because they are most likely to express God's mind, rather than what they say God should have thought.

To presume to act as a prophet in the sense of Jesus and John, we must give evidence of our self-control, mortification, prayer and devotion to solitude. We cannot speak the word of God until we have learned his mind. It would be tendentious to speak for God if he were a stranger to us—or worse, if we should happen to be a sinner. Unlike Elijah, our sinfulness is the only kind of mantle we can be sure has fallen on us.

THIRD WEEK OF ADVENT

Third Sunday of Advent, A

Is 35:1-6, 10; Jas 5:7-10; Mt 11:2-11

By the third Sunday of Advent, I find it hard to hold out and keep thinking "purple" somber thoughts of penance and death. Everyone is waiting for the gold, glitter and lights to break through on Christmas and illuminate the darkness we all experience in life. Even the rose-colored vestments often used on this Sunday do not help me to see the world through rose-colored glasses.

The words of St. James in the second reading are appropriate, *"Be patient, therefore, brothers, until the coming of the Lord."* He cites the patience of farmers, some of whom have to work well into the winter to complete the harvest. He finishes the exhortation by saying, *"Take as an example of hardship and patience, brothers, the prophets who spoke in the name of the Lord."*

The rose vestments represent a modified or toned-down purple, symbolic of our taking a break from penitential fasting and prayer. This Sunday is a rest on our Advent pilgrimage, as if we had reached a landing on the stairway to heaven. The words of the entrance antiphon reflect the mood: *"Rejoice in the Lord."* As week by week another candle is lit on the Advent wreath, we are supposed to be increasing our eagerness for the Light of the World, Jesus. But if the season of violet makes no difference in our lives, the whole message of the liturgy has eluded us. There would be little reason or justification for us to rejoice at Christmas.

St. James once again proposes both farmers and prophets as models of patience and expectation. Even if you don't read the *Farmers' Almanac*, you still have the lovely texts of Isaiah to help you understand prophetic patience.

Although Isaiah uses figures of speech from nature and the outdoors to define the plenty that results from the Lord's coming—the desert in bloom and the flowers of Mount Carmel—the biographical data extant about this prophet reveals that Isaiah was a "city" prophet. We learn that he was married, had at least two sons and fulfilled his ministry as prophet for forty years.

Isaiah was involved in politics and the intrigues of the royal court, as he watched the Jewish kings on a collision course with salvation history. Anyone who has had to deal with government apathy and bureaucratic delays certainly learns to be patient.

All the Near Eastern nations lived at that time in the shadow of Assyria and sooner or later had to decide whether to fight them or submit to their hegemony. There was a long succession of coalitions, alliances and treaties, not unlike the conditions of Israel and the Arab States today. Isaiah repeatedly told his fellow-citizens to trust God, not political alliances. But part of God's demand was a change of heart, to which especially the rulers were not amenable. The analogy for our own country is to solve our own moral evils at home before we presume to set straight the rest of the world. Political and financial deals in high places, pornography, abortion, corruption of ministers of religion, the arms race, pollution of our environment—these are enough for "starters." Actually the prosperity of many citizens may be a curse, especially if it derives from dishonesty or indifference to the poor. What profit is there in gaining the whole world and losing one's soul?

As a "city" prophet rather than a "desert" or "country" prophet, Isaiah linked his preaching and politics to Temple worship. Because the *shekinah*, which means "the glory of the Lord" in Hebrew, resided in the Jerusalem Temple, Isaiah believed that fidelity to its ritual and to the divine presence would together assure military prowess and victory. Yet beautiful liturgies and an artistic environment do not automatically change our hearts.

We find a totally different prophet in John the Baptist, who wouldn't set foot in a city and preferred to roam the hills and deserts of Judea. That was where he knew he belonged—in austerity, privation and prayer. Depending on God and friendly Bedouins for handouts, he wore scratchy mohair and dined on locusts deepfried in olive oil and dipped in wild honey. God chose his messengers and his forerunner, not on the basis of culture, but on the basis of holiness and openness to his word.

The Baptist sent his followers to ask whether Jesus was the Messiah. Jesus feared that the disciples of the abrasive and assertive Baptist might be looking for a political liberator from the Romans. In this matter, Jesus had to be the spiritual director of his cousin John. However, Jesus did not want to deny his own status nor disappoint his forerunner. Therefore, he cited the words of Isaiah about the signs of the messianic age: *"The blind regain their sight, the lame walk,...the poor have the good news preached to them."* The list of messianic activities includes not just physical maladies being cured, but also the healing of the spiritually blind and morally crippled—conditions in which we all may share at times.

Jesus' words about John give us both praise and a mandate. Even though John was the greatest man in history until that time, we who belong to the new kingdom of God are superior to him. We are superior, not in importance to salvation history or necessarily in holiness, but in being knowledgeable about the mysteries of Jesus, the sacraments, the Real Presence, the privileges of Mary, the Holy Trinity and so forth.

So keep up your hopes. Cling yet to your Advent purple; be patient as a farmer waiting for the rain, sun and harvest. Be as disciplined as a prophet and as uncompromising as the Baptist. Be worthy of your mandate and your initiation into the mysteries of the kingdom as a follower of Jesus Christ.

Third Sunday
of Advent, B

Is 61:1-2, 10-11;
1 Thes 5:16-24; Jn 1:6-8, 19-28

As we prepare for the birth of Jesus, we become less threatened by the terrifying God of the Old Testament, who seemed to intervene in human affairs only in crisis situations. In the Child of Bethlehem, God is so approachable and gentle. By his taking on of our humanity, he no longer enters our personal histories only in crisis situations. We never have to feel alone again. Most of all, we have the confidence that we can live forever. His presence is medicine for all of Adam's posterity.

Isaiah prophesied of Jesus in the first reading: *"He has sent me to bring glad tidings to the lowly, to heal the brokenhearted, To proclaim liberty to the captives and release to the prisoners."* You may be a prisoner of sin, brokenhearted because of false friends, a captive in your career or marriage. You may feel lowly and put down by situations over which you have no control. Allow Jesus to enter your life; deliver control over to him. Submit to his governance and listen to his voice.

The second reading from First Thessalonians reiterates, *"The one who calls you is faithful, and he will also accomplish it."* You do not have to be alone. You will remain alone only if you choose separation from God. But you must make an attempt to shake off your lethargy and judge what God's will might be: *"Test everything; retain what is good. Refrain from every kind of evil."*

Jesus has appeared in the form of a servant, as we read in Philippians 2, so that we lose our fear and understand that the Lord himself has shown the way to struggle with evil around us. When Jesus was born, he himself became our way. It was not some modern theologian who first said, "The glory of God is man alive." It was a Father of the Church from the second generation after St. John the Apostle, Irenaeus of Lyons. In fact, Irenaeus goes further to say, "The life of man is the vision of God" *(Against Heresies,* Book IV, 5-7).

The three gospels for the years A, B and C share two themes: rejoice always in the Lord and John the Baptist is the forerunner of the Lord. It is as if the liturgy were telling us to show that we are happy to be followers of the Way and that we are called to make straight the Lord's way into our lives.

This time of year is filled with poetry and metaphors: the root of Jesus, a bride bedecked with her jewels, a voice crying out in the wilderness, windings made straight, a winnowing-fan to clear the threshing floor. Later in his life, Jesus will appeal to similar figures of speech. So the texts of Advent are meant to capture our minds, move our wills and stimulate our hearts. In fact, the whole universe is a figure of speech, because all of creation is a metaphor of God's very being, including ourselves, who are made in the image and likeness of God.

Every good poet should be theologically correct and every theologian must be a poet—to understand the mind of God who has spoken to us in metaphors. Yet there is some danger that we might concentrate on the literature instead of the inspired writing. We could come to the crib and stable, envision singing angels and cuddly lambs and leave this scene unchanged ourselves and lacking in appreciation of correct theology. We should not merely celebrate the nativity as we would attend a play or musical. No, we must have the mindset that the Christmas holiday is happening for the first time and that we are not just spectators, but participants. (That is the whole point of the Mass: the death of Jesus is re-presented mystically as if for the first time.) So every year we enter the stable with the idea that we are witnessing the New Arrival for the first time. We kneel in awe and worship in song. We bring the gifts of a virtuous life, then go to spread on earth the wonder we have seen for the first time.

The theological lesson is twofold: Jesus arrives first of all to give maximum glory to his Father. Secondly, he brings the peace of redemption to this sinful earth. Indeed, the music we should be hearing inside our minds is not sweet violins and jingle bells, but cannons and seventy-six trombones.

Somewhere, in his beautiful writings, G.K. Chesterton said that Jesus came in the morning of humanity when there was a "caveman" mentality—grab, kill, survive. Jesus brings us a new morality of the cave—give, love, die. He comes not in power, but in weakness, not with manipulation, but in supplication. Yes, Jesus begs us to be reborn with him in lowliness and service.

During Advent many families are buying Christmas trees. Although pagan in its origin, the Christmas tree also carries a truthful kind of poetry for the holiday. It is cut off, uprooted, severed and ultimately killed to create a fantasy. So Jesus is destined to die, too. He asks us to be willing to be uprooted from earthbound values, cut off from sin and severed from our old ways of doing things. This is a much truer sign of Christmas than planning holiday menus, wrapping gifts and cutting down on your Christmas card list.

We should already be looking for the star and the prophecies that lead to Bethlehem, straightening out our lives to give access to Jesus. When we are in a hurry and have no car to reach our destination, we can either wait for a bus, which will take us by a circuitous route to our goal, or we can run to catch a taxi and get there in a hurry. With Christmas so close and Bethlehem's meaning still so far away, start running now to be present in person in the cave.

Now is the time to be reborn, in a sense, to your family and friends, whom God has given you to love most on this earth. It is ironic that we are sometimes the most unfeeling towards those we expect to accept us as we are. Your gifts must include yourself; that is the ultimate charity. Unless you give yourself, you have really given nothing. Tell people you love them now, while they are still alive. Put your affection into words and allow the courage of that sentiment to remain throughout the year. At least start with such a resolution. When you unwrap your gifts, stay wrapped up in each other. Don't forget "the reason for the season"—that Gift wrapped in swaddling clothes!

Third Sunday of Advent, C

Zeph 3:14-18; Phil 4:4-7; Lk 3:10-18

Of all the texts concerning John the Baptist, none is so practical and down to earth as today's Gospel. It teaches us clearly how to prepare for the Savior. When questioned by his listeners about their lifestyle, the Baptist does not tell them—"laypersons" of that time— to run off to a monastery, begin large-scale projects for God, or start fasting in an unrealistic way. He simply told the tax collectors (who are necessary to govern any society), *"Stop collecting more than what is prescribed."* He does not appear to call them to heroic actions, such as selling all their possessions for the poor. He invites them to be just plain honest. To the soldiers (likewise neces- sary to keep order and defend a nation) he said, *"Do not practice extortion, do not falsely accuse anyone, and be satis- fied with your wages."* Even though the soldiers were probably the army occupying Palestine, he did not raise the question of a just war, but a just life. He realized that we have to begin small and work into the greater virtues and difficult decisions. The latter would become the message of Christ, soon to begin his public preaching.

The theology of Christmas-coming is profound, yet uncomplicated. The shepherds will receive a sign: a child crying in its mother's arms, helpless and hungry. On Christmas we need not look to speculation and proofs, but simply to accept the mystery of a Child—a God easy to understand, gentle and not threatening. Mary and Joseph surely did not tell the shepherds to overturn their lives. God did not exact a heavy commit- ment from them. He just asked them to respond to the call of the angels and investigate the truth, to come just to wonder at the goodness of God and be accessible to his inspirations.

Each of us is partially crippled and broken because of our sins, hangups, illnesses, griefs and failures. Not only do we need God, but we also need each other. As the shepherds gave little more than the gift of their presence to Jesus, so we can make time for others, especially during our busy preparations for the holidays. Be attentive to others; listen to them. In the second reading to the Church at Philippi St. Paul tells us to be happy. *"Your kindness should be known to all. The Lord is near. Have no anxiety at all.... Then the peace of God that surpasses all understanding will guard your hearts and minds in Christ Jesus."* What marvelous advice during this hectic season of the year.

Our *presence* must always be our main gift. Perhaps that is why a telephone call is better than a card. It is amazing how parents worry about leaving a sizeable estate to their children. Parents fear that disputes frequently could lead to a divided family. The legacy of presence is far more important. This presence lingers in the lives of children after parents are gone, because of the moral influence and the lessons of service to God and neighbor. Jesus gives us a clear lesson: as the Second Person of the Godhead, he needed nothing and nobody. Yet he chose to be like us in all things but sin. He chose each one of us before the world began. Every soul was created individually with some task to perform, so that having completed our task and "completed" ourselves, we might join his eternal celebration.

Sometimes parents, in fact, can be hazards to the spiritual lives of their children. They deter them from a vocation, urge them to "get ahead" of others, make large amounts of money and so forth. But we cannot forget the message of the Christmas Babe and how he died to convalidate his teaching. He upset people, especially the religious leaders of his day and now calls us out of mediocrity. In his "new morality of the cave" he tells us to embrace all people and shake loose of our biases and prejudices. You may never become a missionary or convert scores of people, but you can change your own little corner of the world. Like St. Joseph, you might never even live to see the effectiveness of your spiritual efforts and prayers. But you can give the gift of your presence to the guilty by forgiving them with a sincere heart. You can give your presence to the brokenhearted by cheering those who suffer from being jobless, insecure or sick. You can give your presence to the grief-stricken by encouraging them with words of faith and moral support. You can give your presence to the rejected by looking into their eyes and telling them that they have value and personal importance. You can give your presence to the poor by helping them with food, shelter and maybe a job.

Of course, this world is sometimes awful, but it is also filled with awe at the greatest Presence of all, *Immanuel*, "God with us." He gave us his presence first in Bethlehem (which means "house of bread") and now in the Bread of Life, the Holy Eucharist, the Real Presence. Jesus came an infinite distance from heaven to earth. We have to go only to the nearest church. He did not send a card; he came in person. He does not make great demands, but does ask us to give him our whole heart.

Monday of the Third Week of Advent

Num 24:2-7, 15-17;
Mt 21:23-27

Despite this being an Advent reading, the Gospel scene is related to the passion and death of the Lord. As his end approached, Jesus entered Jerusalem, the place of his suffering. It seemed as if the gentleness and sweetness of his beloved Galilee had ceded to the harsh reality of the Judean terrain. Many scholars have noted that Jesus was typically compassionate and gentle in the north, where Galilee lies. The northern countryside is fertile and beautiful. There he worked his miracles of mercy. There he drew upon nature for his homely metaphors. Going south into the barren land around Jerusalem, Jesus seemed almost to have entered a different mindset. He was more intense and distressed, no doubt fully aware that his end was at hand.

Jesus seemed to disregard the applause, the cries of *Hosanna* and the cloaks and branches thrown under his feet. Realizing the fickleness of the crowd, Jesus' first act was to purify the Temple, his Father's house. He drove out the entrepreneurs of the sacrifices. The exigencies of buying animals and changing foreign coins into shekels made this trafficking necessary. But to prevent commercializing worship, Jesus wanted it done elsewhere.

Evil starts looking all right when enough people stop thinking it's wrong. That was how the money-changers and sellers won acceptance in the Temple precincts: by custom.

After purifying the Temple precincts, Jesus cursed the unproductive fig tree, which instantly withered away (cf. Mt 21:18-22). Alarmed by this invasion of their domain, the chief priests and elders challenged Jesus' right to "take over." Realizing that this was a trap, Jesus countered with his own question about John the Baptist: Did John speak with divine or human authority? If by God's authority, why didn't the priests accept John? If by human authority, then the populace would have been angry, because they considered John a true prophet. Because his opponents disclaimed any knowledge in this matter, Jesus declined to answer. As he continued to expose their hypocrisy, they determined to remove this meddlesome troublemaker. But Jesus eluded capture until his hour arrived at the Passover.

Confrontation is never pleasant and it is natural to avoid painful encounters. Yet our service to God sometimes requires us to stand up for the truth, always provided that we are certain about possessing the truth. Thus we neither back away from truth, as when members of our family are rejecting true values, nor rationalize away guilty actions and surrender principles.

Because we do not have divine insight, we are not free to impute moral guilt (nor even virtue) to others. When we do not know the state of soul of another, it is not appropriate to designate anyone a saint or sinner. The way to assess another is by the kind of enemies he has—the corrupt religious leaders in the case of Jesus. The way to know another is from what he says about others rather than what he claims about himself. Jesus likened the commercial enterprises to a *"den of thieves,"* because zeal for the house of God consumed him.

It is not Christ's way to go under cover and pretend all is well. It is not his way to be willing to tolerate error, stupidity or bad will. Whether the organism is the Body of Christ or the local body politic, we need to keep it healthy and honest. Sometimes cancers are not immediately visible, but we had better pray for guidance and "surgical skill," so we can discern what is truly malignant and what is merely ugly in the Church, what is heresy and what is merely bad taste.

Tuesday of the Third Week of Advent

Zeph 3:1-2, 9-13; Mt 21:28-32

One of the reasons Jesus exasperated the religious leaders is that he saw through their subterfuges. He noticed especially that they laid burdens on others which they were not equal to bearing themselves. They multiplied regulations and handed down explanations of God's laws which only complicated the life of ordinary people. Behind the mask of piety they had their secret sins and private vices. Apparently they did not always practice what they preached.

Nevertheless, in another text Jesus told his followers to obey the leaders of the nation without imitating their laxity. "Do not act as they do, but do as they tell you" (Mt

23:3). We ought not to think, however, that all the leaders were corrupt or hypocritical, because elsewhere in the gospels we read that some Sanhedrin members, such as Nicodemus, believed in Jesus (cf. Jn 3:1-21).

In his dialogue with the priests, Jesus presented the story of a father of two sons. The eldest promised to work in the family vineyard, but lazed around the house instead. The second, younger son complained about the assignment, but thought better of it and did his father's will. Jesus made the unflattering comparison: The elder son represented the self-righteous religious leaders who promised to live by spiritual values, then refused to honor their original commitment. The younger obedient son represented the prostitutes and tax collectors, who at first declined to obey God's law, then had second thoughts and converted.

It is not words and promises, but actions and fulfillment that count. As we say, talk is cheap and actions speak louder than words. When we claim repentance and a change of heart, only time can verify the conversion. The works of penance, of course, essentially refer to reparation, restitution and restoration.

This is the sacrifice God seeks: Restore what you have taken from your neighbor or your employer. Restore the good name you have demeaned and now speak well of that person. Withdraw your negative statements and apologize. Restore what you have not shared with the poor because of your consumerism, exploitation and misuse of the earth's resources. Restore the pride and dignity you have stolen from others by despising them or putting down those who look, act or speak differently than you do. Restore the good cheer and happiness you took from others by your carping, critical and depressing remarks. Restore the religious feelings and sentiments of faith you stole from others by your disparaging comments about religion, religious persons and Church activities. Restore the damage you have done by promising to work in your Father's vineyard to compensate for perhaps years of neglect.

Avoid those persons who can bring you down: negative, exploitative, uncharitable, arrogant and critical associates. A proverb has it: whoever lies down with dogs gets up with fleas. Don't take a chance on swallowing poison, just because you heard about an antidote.

Wednesday of the Third Week of Advent

Is 45:6-8, 18, 21-25;
Lk 7:18-23

In the parlance of John the Baptist, *"the one who is to come"* referred to the Messiah, the Anointed of the Lord. Jesus, on the other hand, may have felt that his bare affirmation of his messiahship would have been insufficient. Therefore he offered some proof of his mission, the signs of the messianic age: cures, resurrection and preaching, as recorded by Isaiah the prophet. In chapter 4 of Luke Jesus cited the same Isaian text (cf. Isaiah 61) in his inaugural homily in the synagogue of Nazareth, his hometown, where he began his evangelization.

No doubt there was an ancillary reason to quote Isaiah against the popular expectations that the Messiah would conquer by force and eject the Roman war machine by military strategems. Yet this was outside the divine commission from his Father.

John the Baptist, the fiery and charismatic preacher, may not have understood this himself and may have wondered why Jesus had not entered the Holy City in a blaze of glory to take over the Temple, his Father's house. There he was, quietly and peaceably wandering around Galilee with no thought of David's royal throne. He preached mildness and submission to authority. Jesus' response was to teach John and his disciples the truth about his Father's mandate.

"And blessed is the one who takes no offense at me." An earlier translation reads, "who is not scandalized in me." This remark was directed at Jesus' own followers as well as at John's. The important spiritual point is that we must accept Jesus on his own terms and with his specific teachings and message. We cannot accept him as we envision him, not as we have preconceived his role. This fact holds good today as well. It is a kind of idolatry to make him over according to our own image or our expectation, as if we were the measure of his mission.

It is spiritually dangerous and certainly fruitless to interpose our own egotistical ideas between ourselves and God. We may try to manipulate the Lord to grant us favors, to complete our agenda and to regulate our personal history as we decide it must be. We may even ask that he convert others to our way of thinking and so forth.

We may conceivably be praying for laudable goals such as a change of heart for some family member, reconciliation of hostile neighbors and finding a needed job. We must realize that God's schedule of timing and agenda differs from our own. He does not violate the free will that makes us characteristically human. Freedom to obey and love necessarily include the opposite choices.

A person takes offense at and is scandalized by Jesus when he or she gives up prayer or the proper practices of religion. Such a person finds that God is not conforming to his or her concept of a beneficent deity. Actually God always hears our prayers and always answers. It is just that his answer is often a clear "no."

Thursday of the
Third Week of Advent

Is 54:1-10;
Lk 7:24-30

Today's Gospel continues yesterday's encounter with the inquisitive, ubiquitous, persistent disciples of the Baptist. Jesus clearly praised John and his baptism of repentance. He himself had been baptized by his cousin, John. The text closes with the satisfaction of the bystanders who had themselves received John's baptism. At least some of the lawyers and Pharisees had really *"rejected the plan of God for themselves"* by refusing to be baptized. The encomium by Jesus indicates that John was the hinge between the prior religious tradition— the Jewish Testament—and the future promise, the Christian Testament.

Jesus reminded the crowds that his cousin John was the precursor, his forerunner, the "messiah" of the Messiah. John's imprisonment for criticizing Herod should not have shaken his followers, because that is the destiny of most prophets. John's disciples did, after all, consider him to be Elijah-returned-to-earth. He was a prophet in the grand tradition of Judaism, a desert dweller. He was physically and morally strong and indefatigable. John was beholden to no one, treating everyone with equal abrasiveness when necessary. Yet better is an honest slap than a false kiss. We would all prefer the concern of a sincere criticism than the indifference of unexpressed affection. Someone added to the phrase of St. John, "The truth shall make you free—and often embarrassed."

John the Baptist was no wimp, no weak-kneed *"reed swayed by the wind"* of public opinion and popularity polls. He neither ate nor dressed like those who *"are found in royal palaces"* and the political centers of power. In fact, Jesus said, he was more than a prophet. Of those

THIRD WEEK OF ADVENT   77

"born of women, no one is greater than John." This encouragement no doubt made these inquirers amenable to Jesus' message.

The concluding comparison, however, was more a praise of Jesus' followers and a cause of wonder and perhaps confusion to his listeners. *"Yet the least in the kingdom of God is greater than John."* The members of the new creation, born of water and the Holy Spirit, are co-heirs with Jesus, their brother under God, in the eternal kingdom. Not only is heaven's gate open to them, but already on earth they are privy to the mysteries of redemption. They have access to their heavenly Father through Jesus.

We are called to be John the Baptist for others: to prepare Jesus' coming into their hearts, to be the catalyst in their reaction with the Savior. Simultaneously, we must decrease while Jesus increases in them, taking over their lives and transforming them into his likeness. We see this phenomenon of John's decrease in the Gospel. At first John is actively preaching at the Jordan and even baptizes Jesus. Next he is shown in prison at a distance from the "action" of Jesus. Further, he is seen only through his disciples making inquiry of Christ, as in today's text. Finally, we get the report of his beheading. His annihilation is complete.

We are seldom called to resist evil and stand up for good to the degree that the Baptist manifested by his life and death. Yet God does not excuse us from decreasing, especially our own egos, so he may increase his influence, grace and love in the world.

Friday of the
Third Week of Advent

Is 56:1-3, 6-8;
Jn 5:33-36

We can always depend on John the evangelist to lift us from our pedestrian way of thinking to fly with him to theological heights. This section of his Gospel cites the witnesses to the validity of Jesus' claims that he came down from heaven. The witnesses are Jesus' works, the testimony of our heavenly Father and the very Bible itself. Jesus also names John the Baptist as his witness.

Jesus convicted his hearers of the sin of being content with John's teachings only for a while, but the word of God did not abide in their hearts. Moreover they refused to believe him whom *"the Father has sent."* Thus Jesus asserted that his light exceeds the small-flamed lamp that was the Baptist. Jesus was the independent light, set on fire by no mere earthly source. He was the gushing flow of life-giving water, which is what he called the Holy Spirit.

Of all the "witnesses" to the veracity and validity of his mission, Jesus favors his own *"works,"* assigned to him by his heavenly Father, as the clearest index to his messiahship. Jesus was sent to heal and teach, bless and lift up, raise the dead and preach to the poor. Thus the ultimate endorsement comes through faith in Jesus as teacher and healer. This faith is a pure and simple gift to which no one is naturally entitled.

Faith is an interior witness. Neither the accumulation of "proofs" nor all the intellectual arguments in the world serve as reliable "witnesses" to Jesus. Only what he accomplishes in souls suffices to make us believe in him. Jesus himself did not stress his works of wonder. He frequently commanded the beneficiaries of his healing power not to publish these deeds or praise him publicly. He did not wish to depend in his mission on the startling and extraordinary. He asked for faith in his message, a contrite heart, generous aid to the poor, unceasing prayer, detachment from this world. This is faith in his messiahship: healing of one's soul, cure of the heart and the resurrection of long-forgotten virtues.

Jesus sends his Spirit upon his converts to convict the world of sin (cf. Jn 16:8). He teaches us what to say during harassment and how to speak with God. He tells us how to cry out with affection, *"Abba, Father"* (Mk 14:36) as a child trustingly and lovingly runs to his earthly parent for security, nourishment and love.

Christians should reflect more about their call to holiness. Without shame they can share with others the favors the Lord has bestowed on them. They can teach others how to achieve intimacy with God in prayer. Thus they become part of the "witness" of the Church to Christ. The Body of Christ is perennially in a state of tension or even crisis. Every age thinks its own conflicts are the worst in history. But the Church must carefully balance between order and chaos: form as well as shapelessness both have drawbacks if either is emphasized too much.

The Church's consistent problem historically has been to maintain the centrist position between liberty that verges on libertinism and a conservative posture which canonizes the past for its own sake. The difficulty is compounded in a pluralistic society such as our own where diversity is generally applauded and in a democratic nation where leaders require a popular mandate. Yet there is a constant urgency to maintain traditional values and rediscover our past. The Church escapes the excesses of these conflicts by adherence to the "tried, tested, and true," which we call Tradition.

FOURTH SUNDAY OF ADVENT

Fourth Sunday of Advent, A

Is 7:10-14;
Rom 1:1-7; Mt 1:18-24

The beginning of Matthew's Gospel is eminently the history of the foster father of Jesus. Because Matthew is writing for converted Jews, the neophyte Christians, he keeps returning to the Jewish antecedents of Christ. The Savior fulfills the Jewish prophecies regarding the Messiah: He is the new Moses and Son of David. He is the promised Messiah, the spiritual freedom fighter. For a Jew one's heritage was traced on the paternal side, not the maternal. Therefore, Joseph's role assumes great weight in Matthew, just as Mary's role supersedes Joseph's in Luke's Gospel.

How noble was Joseph! No wonder some spiritual writers consider him second only to Mary among us human beings in importance, grace and privilege. He had a wife but didn't have her. He had a son but didn't exactly have a son. Yet as adoptive parents and children know, the real mother and father are those who nurture, cherish, love and raise their adoptive children. Anyone can be a biological parent but mothering and fathering take a variety of skills.

Joseph sums up the best instincts of the Jewish Testament, the Old Law. As a devout Jew, he knew the prophecies about the Messiah. He was asked by God through an angel to sacrifice his life on the often-bitter altar of chaste celibacy. He surely fantasized—and properly so—about marriage with this lovely daughter of Sion, Mary. No doubt he always loved her with all his great heart, if only from a distance. He looked forward to siring his own children, sweet and beautiful girls and strong and manly sons to stand at his side. He was probably in the prime of his life, not a white-bearded old man as he is sometimes depicted in Christian art. God needed a man to protect Jesus and Mary throughout their Egyptian sojourn.

There are many apocryphal stories about St. Joseph. ("Apocryphal" means "hidden," that is, written sources that developed without known authors.) Through Jesus, Joseph had a closer contact with God than the ancient Jewish patriarchs and prophets. Some stories claim that his body never corrupted after death (although no one knows where he is buried). It is also a reasonable belief that Joseph died in the arms of Jesus and Mary. No wonder that he is invoked as the patron of a happy death. One scarcely credible legend has it that Joseph had six sons by a prior marriage with a wife who died when Joseph was eighty-nine years old. Only then, says the legend, did he marry our Lady.

It has often been said that the Bible is the history of both heroes and villains. Joseph is an authentic hero, a noble model for all believers, but especially for fathers and husbands, for laborers and devout believers. He taught Jesus not only his trade and craft of carpentry, but also his spiritual lessons as a Jewish boy. Surely Joseph felt proud to have Jesus sit next to him in their local synagogue and at his *Bar-mitzvah*.

For our sake, Matthew recorded Joseph's anxiety over Mary's pregnancy. The evangelist encourages us in our difficulties. Even the best of us may doubt, that is, become confused over our difficulties at times. Here Joseph was contending with a brand new concept: a virgin-mother by God's intervention. Joseph is a model for everyone with a special personal vision. He is the model for someone trying to take hold of a dream, someone in need of trust and hope. Exposing Mary *"to shame"* meant she could be stoned to death for apparent adultery, so Joseph intended to divorce her quietly until the angel intervened.

Joseph was told to name the Baby. In Luke, Mary is told her Baby's name by the angel Gabriel (cf. Lk 1:31). In antiquity when a man conferred the name on a child, this was a sign that he accepted the paternity of that child, whether biologically or by adoption. Matthew is once more reinforcing the "Jewishness" of Jesus, the Son of David.

In the second reading, St. Paul wrote to the Church at Rome that Jesus was made *"Son of God in power,"* but was *"descended from David according to the flesh."* This places the first reading from Isaiah in perspective. David's descendant and Jesus' ancestor was King Ahaz, a young man on the throne, incapable of coping with the politics of the eighth century B.C. The Jewish kingdom was surrounded by enemies. With the help of Syria, Judah's sister-kingdom of Israel in the north was pressing down upon it. Ahaz was being harassed also by Assyria from the Fertile Crescent to the east to submit, pay tribute, or be liquidated.

Isaiah told Ahaz not to rely on political alliance, but to trust in God. In fact, he was told to ask God for some sign. In a pretense of piety, King Ahaz refused to ask for a sign. Exasperated, Isaiah told him the sign anyway and admonished him to listen and to stop wearying God.

"The virgin shall be with child, and bear a son, and shall name him Immanuel." We are not sure what that meant immediately to Ahaz, but we understand it in the light of Christ.

Jesus was never called "Immanuel" in the Bible. In Hebrew the name means "God (is) with us." Thus more than just a name, *Immanuel* states a function of Jesus: to be God among human beings, to be the manifestation of the *shekinah*. No longer could mankind say that God was distant, apart from human affairs, separate from history. He is one of us. He became a man, as the Fathers put it, so that we might become "gods" through participation in his nature, so as to inherit heaven.

Fourth Sunday of Advent, B

2 Sm 7:1-5, 8-11, 16;
Rom 16:25-27; Lk 1:26-38

The first reading is from 2 Samuel, a historical book of the Bible. Though intensely interesting, the staid language of 2 Samuel conceals a hot dialogue between heaven and earth. Let us try to reconstruct the text in more familiar terms. King David, who was human and weak at times in light of his many transgressions, said to the court prophet, Nathan: *"Here I am living in a house of cedar, while the ark of God dwells in a tent!"* The ark was miles from the Holy City of Jerusalem in a town that today is called Abu Gosh. In modern expression, David would say: "Nathan, get on the hot line with God. I'll tell you what I am going to do. I will build a temple right next to my royal palace on this hill."

We can surmise that when God heard the deal, he probably replied to Nathan: "Build me a temple? He should live so long. I made him the commander of the Jewish armies. I helped him slay Goliath when he was a boy. I gave Saul's throne to him. He was a nobody, just an unknown shepherd boy. I know what his hidden agenda is: he wants my temple next to his house, so that the other tribes of Israel have to come to his capital city and he can control them."

Then the Lord God must have considered his own Son and softened his tone. "Your temple I don't need," he told David, through Nathan, "but I will preserve your name and posterity. I will be a father to all your descendants" (cf. 2 Sm 7:16). This is, of course, a prediction about Jesus, who took our human nature at the Annunciation. Today's Gospel records the fulfillment of God's promise to David through Nathan.

Christian art generally depicts Mary at prayer when the Archangel Gabriel appeared before her. Often she has the Jewish Bible open before her and she is kneeling. Nevertheless, a local tradition in Nazareth, even today, is that she was drawing water at the well. The Arab population still calls the well by her name. It is also still being used as a source of water. Others say that she had already taken the jar of water home to do the dishes or to begin supper. Because Gabriel said, *"Do not be afraid, Mary,"* she was undoubtedly taken aback.

Was she perhaps not at prayer? Who knows for sure? We dare not take away the humanness from the Holy Family, nor their anxieties amid daily activities. Mary kept house before the days of vacuum cleaners and microwave ovens. The point is that in the midst of scrubbing, sweeping, cooking, weaving and washing, she took the time to listen for God's voice and was ready to answer when he spoke. She did this better than anyone else who ever lived.

Then her problems started. She became pregnant outside wedlock when she was only a teenager. She had to be worried about what Joseph, her intended, as well as her parents might say. Of course, there is no record of any angel appearing to Joachim and Anne. How would you react if your pregnant, unwed daughter were to say, "Don't worry. My child will be the Son of the Most High. I heard that from an angel!" Thus human problems were not absent from those "golden moments" surrounding the first Christmas. This Gospel appears before the holy day, so that we are fully aware of the demands of faith upon Joseph and Mary.

Therefore, do not think that your religious practices will absolve you of problems. Only your faith can accomplish that. God guarantees that you will have sufficient help if you submit to his will (as you can best understand it for the present), correspond to grace and use your practical insights. As you wind down your Advent pilgrimage, learn, like Mary, to find God in ordinary things, in down-to-earth activities. They have become important in the Christian dispensation only because the Son of God sanctified them as part of his own family life on earth. In a simple metaphor: faith is not an aspirin; it is a vitamin pill.

Fourth Sunday
of Advent, C

Mi 5:1-4; Heb 10:5-10;
Lk 1:39-45

Micah, the prophet-author of the first reading, said, "*But you, Bethlehem-Ephrathah, too small to be among the clans of Judah, From you shall come forth for me one who is to be ruler in Israel;...his greatness shall reach to the ends of the earth; he shall be peace.*" Imagine the Jews of old who heard this prophecy. The great king was to be born in dry and dusty Bethlehem, a small cluster of stone and mud huts and caves off the beaten track. Bethlehem was too small to be the center or mini-capital of a clan, which was a minor subdivision of a tribe.

Many texts of Scripture carry this theme: What man considers small, God considers important. He often acted through those who were spiritually weak, power-less and lacking natural ability. Jeremiah protested at being called to be a prophet: "I am too young; I do not know how to speak" (Jer 1:6). God tells Gideon to con-quer the Midianites who were harassing the Jews, but he replies, "My family is the lowest in the tribe of Man-asseh" (Jgs 6:15). Saul tells Samuel who is supposed to anoint him king, "My clan is the least among the clans of the tribe of Benjamin" (1 Sm 9:21). David was the youngest son of Jesse, sent off with the sheep into pas-ture. St. Paul felt helpless when he wrote to the Church at Corinth: "God singled out the weak to shame the strong" (1 Cor 1:27). "When I am powerless, it is then that I am strong" (2 Cor 12:10). It seems that littleness is important to God.

Most of all, as we prepare for a baby's arrival, we should celebrate the theme of littleness. "A child shall lead them" (Is 11:6). Then there is Micah alluding to the non-importance of Bethlehem. What irony. The Roman Empire, proud and mighty, governor of millions of lives, thought it was running the world. Caesar decreed a census probably for tax purposes. Thus Mary and Jo-seph had to register in David's village, because Joseph was from the family and house of David. Through that census, the whole Empire was made a part of God's plan. The machinery of government was spinning with-out any awareness of being used by heaven. In this way, little Bethlehem could become "big" Bethlehem. Peas-ants and carpenters with dirt under their fingernails were not important to emperors, except for taxation. The Roman rulers mentally divided the population into the powerful and the indigent. But we see that "nobodies" can count.

When you visit an Indian village in Mexico, you really get the feel of Bethlehem. Due to lack of govern-ment personnel and funds, the Indians, especially in remote places, are neglected. There are few schools in the hinterland. Houses, generally without windows, are built of adobe or sticks woven together. Most clothes are made in the home, except where cheap polyester is available. People wear their clothes until they are completely worn out.

The forest provides the "rest rooms" and the river is the bathtub. Running water and electricity are available in larger villages for those who can afford it.

It is rare to see anyone wearing footgear. The cooking is done over wood fires. The same Indian clothing (white pants and a shirt) suffices for a man's work, church, sleep, as well as for his wedding and funeral. Contrary to myths, Indians are not taciturn and stoic. They are lively and responsive, especially if you speak their language and fuss over their children.

Simple people often have practical wisdom and beauty of soul. They honor old age and accept the advice of elders. Everyone is expected to provide some services to the community on a regular basis: to build roads, take care of orphans, clean the church and public square, etc. They try to keep clean by daily bathing in the river— women and children by day and the men by night. They have a great faith in God (even when they don't assist at Mass) and respect for our Lady. The elders (principales) of the tribe meet every week to discuss matters of common importance.

Even though living with such simple people provides less than perfect hygiene, a strange language and odd customs, you can learn from them about simplicity. They are not unhappy because they do not always realize that they are poor, unless they visit a big city. You must accept them as they are and show that you care.

With little change, that pretty well describes Bethlehem. We say to Jesus in a Church canticle, "You did not shrink from the Virgin's womb." He entered our lives and showed a predilection for the poor, the uneducated, sinners, foreigners. He expects us to accept and care about those who have a different color of skin, language, customs and nationality.

As you prepare to celebrate the Child who has done this before us as our model, ask yourself: Do you value the mighty politicians, stars and athletes? Are they your Caesar? Do you, instead, respect the poor as the apple of God's eye, the way Jesus did? Do you try to discover God's plan of establishing his kingdom just as when the Roman empire unknowingly fit into God's master design for salvation? Look to Mary, of whom Elizabeth said, "Blessed is she who trusted that the Lord's word would be fulfilled" (Lk 1:45).

Do not long to be important, wealthy, famous or powerful. In other words, do not be ashamed of your littleness, once you recognize how the Son of God emptied himself and took the form of a slave (cf. Phil 2:7). The big God made himself very small, indeed.

DECEMBER 17-24

December 17

Gn 49:2, 8-10;
Mt 1:1-17

Today in the breviary as well as the texts of the Mass, we begin the final week of preparation for Christmas. We discontinue the regular Advent readings to review all the principal events of salvation history. This includes the Jewish Testament and the infancy narratives of the Christian Testament.

We open with chapter 49 of Genesis, which recalls God's intervention in the tribe of Judah, from which Jesus would be born. At the very beginning of the Bible, when Adam and Eve were being expelled from Eden, God unilaterally promised them a Savior. He also promised the serpent, the devil: "He shall crush your head and you shall lie in wait for his heel" (Gn 3:15). As the human race multiplied and spread, God kept his divine eye on certain persons until he chose Abraham, "our father in faith," to leave his home in Chaldea and begin the trek that would take him along the Fertile Crescent in a big arc that ended in Canaan or Palestine (cf. Gn 12ff.) The gospel genealogy in Matthew continues from Abraham.

In the first reading, old Jacob utters prophecies about the future of his twelve sons. Judah is the particular subject of today's reading. He will be as fierce as a lion and his brothers will bow to him. No one will dare to take away his scepter, the sign of royal power, from his hands. No one will remove the mace, a powerful weapon, from between his legs, where it is positioned for war.

After Solomon the descendants of Judah became the Southern Kingdom. They are the ancestors of modern Jews. The house of David came from Judah and, therefore, so did Jesus. Nevertheless, David's royal lineage did die out. However, the scepter never did depart from Judah, because Jesus spiritually fulfilled the prophecy.

Matthew's Gospel today relates the human ancestry of Jesus, especially his descent from David. Scholars point out that the wording is artificial: three sets of fourteen generations, thereby skipping some ancestors to make the plan work. When numbers are substituted for the Hebrew letters that spell out "David," the sum is fourteen. The point of this contrivance is to connect Jesus with David for the sake of the converts from Judaism.

Already in the second century after Christ, heretics denied the human nature of the Second Person or claimed that Jesus—divine and human—did not die on the cross. Therefore, the infancy narratives of Matthew and Luke contain genealogies that reinforce the humanity of Jesus. This firmly roots Jesus in human history. The Son of God became the son of man, the child of Mary, our brother. He stepped in line behind Adam and Eve and crushed that ancient serpent who seduced our first parents.

December 18

When there is a difficult passage of the Bible, the explanation tends to reflect scholarship more than inspiration. Nevertheless sometimes the writer's message and the spiritual application cannot be understood without presenting the background of his text. In his Jewish way, Matthew continues to show Joseph as the head of the household. What is more, Joseph is recorded as the lineal descendant of King David and (unrealistically by that time) the heir to the throne of Judea. For a moment Joseph appears more important than Jesus or Mary.

To emphasize Jesus as the center of Jewish history and tradition, Joseph has to appear as the key to this text, even though he is the adoptive father. Mary's words are not quoted. She is mentioned only in passing, as if she were merely a silent and passive spectator. (In Luke the reverse is true.) Joseph was *"righteous,"* which means a follower of Jewish law. Yet he tried to manifest his loving concern for his future wife. Like any other man who seemed betrayed by his fiancée, Joseph should have been naturally indignant, even outraged at what was ostensibly her infidelity. Yet he saw her deep prayer life, her modesty and purity and her obvious pain that Joseph was suddenly aware of her being pregnant.

What could Mary have said that would have sounded believable? Would Joseph believe that God caused her condition and the Child was divine? As for the public eye, it was apparently not unusual for a couple to live together, once the marriage contract was struck at the time of engagement, but it was still not typical. Yet until co-habitation Joseph could divorce her *"quietly"* and without revealing his motive. Matthew makes a major point of this to underscore that Mary was a virgin. Exposure to the law would cause her to be accused publicly for the evident sin and probably stoned to death with utter legality. Joseph decided he had to separate from his beloved Mary, but wanted to spare her pain and degradation. He would go to a priest and get a "bill of divorce." And can you imagine the feelings of Joachim and Anna?

When we see the crib with hovering angels, sweet Mary and strong Joseph, adoring shepherds and cuddly lambs, everything seems delightful. But think of it: pregnancy outside marriage, threat of divorce or even stoning, the shame of public opinion looming over the couple, and the impossibility of giving explanations. The coming of Jesus demanded commitment and created many hardships. For us, too, commitment to Jesus often creates confusion and pain. As Mary, we must depend on God to unravel these knots and solve our problems.

December 19

Jgs 13:2-7, 24-25;
Lk 1:5-25

There is a transparent parallel between the stories of Samson in the first reading and John the Baptist in today's Gospel. In both cases, as well as in other Bible stories, the heroes were born of elderly, seemingly sterile parents. Recall that Abraham and Sarah delivered Isaac when they were about one hundred years old (cf. Gn 21:5). No doubt the implication was that such offspring were generated not by carnality, but by obeying the Lord's command to procreate.

Further, both Samson and John were Nazirites, dedicated by their mothers from birth to God's service. With their uncut hair, they looked like wild men. Samson was fierce to the enemy Philistines. He slaughtered them and scattered them until Delilah found the secret of his strength and cut his hair (cf. Jgs 17:19). John slew spiritual enemies and put down men's vices. He verbally attacked Herod, some religious leaders and the unrepentant.

The Gospel provides considerable detail about the birth of the Baptist, partly because of the notoriety of those events surrounding his conception and birth. Zechariah, his father, experienced a vision and was made mute at the altar of incense during the vesper service. All the people wondered what his child might become. Perhaps the baby would even be the long-awaited Messiah.

Another parallel did not escape the Fathers of the Church. Both Samson and John lost their lives in different ways through the seductions of loose women. The story of Delilah is familiar to all and we also remember how Salome danced away the life of John. Salome received the Baptist's head on a platter for her evil mother (cf. Mt 14:3-12). The difference is that Samson got himself into trouble. But his hair grew long again, as a sign of his return to chastity and discipline under the yoke. Thus God's favor returned and he became mighty against the enemies of Israel.

We learn from today's readings that no one should consider himself or herself safe from seduction, compromise and falling from grace. Give Satan an inch and he will take a foot, after which it is all downhill into destruction. Second, it is reasonable to hope against hope, as did Elizabeth and Zechariah, because everything is possible to God. Third, like Samson, who repented and changed himself, it is never too late to say we are sorry and amend our lives.

"Reform" means to put something back into form, back into shape. This implies that we know what the original shape or mold is all about. Today's readings suggest that our desirable mold is both clear and attainable, as far as God is concerned. He makes everything possible and does not command the impossible. The form he wishes to find in us is the likeness to his Son, Jesus.

December 20

Is 7:10-14;
Lk 1:26-38

This Gospel appears several times a year, especially for Marian feasts, perhaps because we cannot get enough of a good thing. The text is so rich in spirituality. After the Madonna and Child, the Annunciation scene is probably the most frequently depicted in Western religious art, painting, stained-glass windows and mosaics.

Whenever I read a Scripture text, my mind and my imagination drift back through salvation history. I wonder about the actions and motivations of the people who participated in these Bible events. I reflect on the boy with the two fish at the miraculous multiplication (cf. Jn 6:9ff.), the Canaanite woman who compared herself to a dog eating the scraps from its master's table (cf. Mk 7:28), the young man who went away sad because he was rich (cf. Mt 19:16-30). I also wonder about what Mary was doing at the Annunciation.

There are wells at the walls of Jerusalem, Bethlehem and Nazareth still referred to as "Mary's well." Was Mary drawing water when the stranger—an archangel—approached her and began that immortal dialogue? No wonder Mary was startled. Strange men did not converse with village maidens, especially when they were unattended. Or did she pull her loom into the yard to get better light on her weaving? Or was she sweeping under the bed and making small piles in the house to pick up at the end of her chore? Or was she praying an ancient psalm of her people? The point is that we never know when God will send a message to us. We must always be expectant, listening, waiting, intent.

The Annunciation forms the opening measures of a symphony with this theme: history climaxes in Jesus. The Gospel today records the central event of human history, the Incarnation itself. Jesus (to use his own words) begins to draw all things to himself (cf. Jn 12:32). Yet all this took place in an otherwise ordinary, typical human family. This is the human aspect that we often overlook. The lesson is that we should seek the divine through and among ordinary events in our lives. The divine investment in our human nature not only emphasizes our dignity as men and women, but also that God is "at home" in lowliness and simplicity.

As a daughter of Sion, a young Jewess, Mary must have had sentiments of patriotism. She must have pined for the coming of the Messiah. The psalmist pined for the courts of the Lord's house (cf. Ps 83:3), and now Mary was about to become the Lord's house. Her womb would be the ark of his covenant. In the fullness of time, when the world is "teachable," at its moment of readiness, God sends his Son to us (cf. Gal 4:4). For God "time" means nothing, whereas "timing" is everything and "timeliness" is where this earth touches heaven. God's messages are, therefore, linked to the peak moments of world history, when earthlings get a momentary glimpse of the divine plan and begin to pine for the courts of the Lord's house.

December 21

Sg 2:8-14 (or) Zep 3:14-18;
Lk 1:39-45

Ein Karim, the modern name of the village of Zechariah and Elizabeth, is in the hill country of Judah. It is about one hundred kilometers or seventy miles from Nazareth. A journey took several days, perhaps a week of walking or riding a donkey ten miles a day. Possibly Mary traveled with Joseph or another chaperone. She had to pass famous sites steeped in Jewish history: battlegrounds, tombs and fortresses. She must have pondered their significance to her people's past, but also to their future in the light of the secret she carried in her womb.

Mary passed the beautiful Plain of Esdraelon, the Valley of Jezreel, not far from Megiddo (or Armageddon) where the final battle between good and evil was supposed to be fought at the endtime (cf. Rv 16:14-16). Mary passed Mt. Gerizim, home of the Samaritans and into Jerusalem, where St. Ann, her mother, is thought to have lived near the Sheep's Gate. Traveling a little further west of the capital, she reached Ein Karim, the ancient name of which has eluded the scholars.

The fact that John the Baptist stirred in Elizabeth's womb has always been interpreted by the theologians to mean that he was sanctified or purified of original sin. In a sense, he was "baptized" by the holy presence of the Savior in Mary's womb. Only Jesus, Mary and John the Baptist were born without sin on their souls. Nevertheless, Jesus would later say of his cousin John that the least in the kingdom of his Father was greater than John (cf. Mt 11:11), because we have a share in the mysteries and life of Christ. Christians are enabled to live on earth in the presence of the Father and in the intimacy of the Holy Spirit.

In Luke's first chapter, Mary is said to have *"pondered"* which means that she "weighed" all these occurrences, so as to mine the treasures of grace given into her keeping. She had to reflect, because only slowly was God revealing the mission of her Son and the way he was working in her. The Gospels were written after all these events, but while they were happening, Mary had to ask herself whether she was doing exactly what God was expecting of her. We, too, must ponder whether we are meeting God's intentions for us. Rarely do human beings receive a direct imperative from God or a heavenly communication from an angel. God's grace is enough for us to figure out his will. Generally, the confusion derives from our unwillingness to perform his will.

The gospels are a summary, not a full history. They present the highlights of salvation history, to which human insights and chronicles must cede. Even though God is working through us, we need to work out our salvation with fear and trembling (cf. Phil 2:12). We cannot be so arrogant to think we have the "inside track" with God. Ask God today to share in Mary's spirit of willing obedience and her attitude of pondering.

December 22

1 Sm 1:24-28;
Lk 1:46-56

Mary's canticle is called the *Magnificat* from the opening word in Latin. The words, spoken to Elizabeth during the Visitation, were not entirely original. So bathed in the Jewish Testament was Mary, that she gave an echo and paraphrase of the canticle of Hannah, mother of Samuel. Hannah's canticle, in fact, is the responsorial psalm for today. After years of barrenness, Hannah conceived Samuel. Her son became the future prophet and mentor of King Saul, the first King of Israel. Similarly, Elizabeth, who had also been barren, conceived the Baptist in her old age.

Some scholars think that the canticle of Mary was a later addition to Luke's narrative inserted by faithful believers. However, since Mary was steeped in Jewish lore and traditions, there is no need to deny her authorship of the *Magnificat*. Mary probably studied, even memorized those passages that particularly relate to the role of women's service to God in the Jewish Bible. Of course, if Mary did not compose this canticle, it is in a sense even more remarkable that Christians from the first century made such important statements about Mary, as *"From now on will all ages call me blessed."*

The *Magnificat* sums up Mary's spirituality. She is among the *anawim*, a special biblical term that describes the perfect servant of God. The *anawim* depend on God because they feel powerless to accomplish any good of themselves. *Anawim* are more likely to be poor and weak, rather than rich and powerful. Yet it is not the absence of wealth and status, but one's mindset or attitude that is the mark of holiness. The rich and powerful also have to save their souls by praying with all their hearts to be submissive to the divine will. The typical stumbling block is that money, power and higher education at times lead to a sense of self-sufficiency.

The canticle's closing words are a prophecy that the promise made to Abraham and his descendants was being fulfilled. The promise was that the children of Abraham would be numberless and never perish from the earth (cf. Gn 22:17-18). God has kept the promise to the Jews in that they have survived in ethnic integrity. He also extends the promise to us in the new covenant, who, as Pope John XXIII said, are "spiritual Semites" and the offspring of Abraham. Our presence will never cease upon this earth. The gates of hell or jaws of death will never overcome us.

Necessary, however, to the fulfillment of the promise is our posture of lowliness and trusting submission as the *anawim*, the poor and helpless of the Lord. This is an attitude born of prayer, matured by perseverance and crowned by the experience of his mercy.

December 23

Mal 3:1-4, 23-24;
Lk 1:57-66

A common Jewish custom surfaces in this reading: At the circumcision ritual, a boy is named after his father, uncle or grandfather. St. Thomas Aquinas considered circumcision the means of being co-opted into God's family. It was the Jewish counterpart or equivalent of Christian Baptism. Thus males were incorporated into the people of the covenant by the quasi-sacrificial shedding of blood. By receiving a name, the child received an identity as a person.

To one of the prophets the Lord said, "By your name I have called you" (Is 43:1). To be given a name in the Temple or synagogue, that is, in the Lord's presence, conferred some share in the Lord's power. On the other hand, God was reluctant to reveal his name even to Moses. Apart from the possibility of blasphemy, knowledge of the name of a deity, it was thought, gave the possessor of that knowledge the right and even the power to invoke the holy name for private uses. In the same way, a Christian can exorcise a demon, heal and baptize in the name of Jesus. The Christian can call upon that holy name to work wonders and even miracles, as did the first disciples.

Knowledge of the marvels attendant upon John the Baptist's conception and birth led the observers to exclaim *"What, then, will this child be?"* and *"For surely the hand of the Lord was with him."* Being an object of wonder and amazement, not to mention curiosity, is very much a part of giving good example. If we are always honest and truthful, hard-working and church-going, others will ask, "How come?" and "What's going on in their lives?" and "What do they know that I don't know?" This is precisely the mystery of grace at work to change us, to heal us, to impel us to greater efforts for the kingdom.

Therefore God asks us to be the cause of wonder to others and to demonstrate his power in our lives. We need to give witness or testimony to his power in work and in word as well. It is seldom the heroic actions that we are asked to present to the world. Nor ought we think that God calls only the pious, devout persons to work significantly for the kingdom.

Throughout salvation history, the lives of the saints reveal amazing conversions from sin and worldliness. We immediately think of the parties of Francis of Assisi and the military carousing of Ignatius Loyola. Nevertheless, most saints remain long on many plateaus of seeming stagnation from the point of their conversion. Even the sudden and startling changes of heart must be repeated often.

None of us at our births probably provoked the question, *"What, then, will this child be?"* But the tenor of our lives and dedication to the kingdom should surely lead others to comment by the end of our earthly journey, "Was not the hand of the Lord upon him?"

December 24
Mass in the Morning

2 Sm 7:1-5, 8-11, 16; Lk 1:67-79

The canticle of Zechariah, John the Baptist's father, invites comparison with Mary's canticle, which appears earlier in the same chapter. Both are very "Jewish" and redolent with its traditions. Both speak of the promise of God to his people. Mary said, "He has upheld Israel his servant, ever mindful of his mercy; even as he promised our fathers, promised Abraham and his descendants forever." Zechariah proclaimed: *"He has raised up a horn for our salvation within the house of David his servant, even as he promised through the mouth of his holy prophets from of old.... the oath he swore to Abraham our father, and to grant us that,... without fear we might worship him."*

Both canticles proclaim God's might in delivering people from their enemies, especially enemies which are proud and arrogant. The worshiper's task is to trust God and praise him, thus giving him glory. God, of course, will continue his wonderful works.

Mary's cause for joy was not only the Incarnation, but her delivery from the impasse of Joseph wishing to divorce her *"quietly."* Zechariah, on the other hand, praised God for delivering Elizabeth from her sterility. We must remember that the old priest had been mute since the encounter with the Archangel Gabriel in the Temple. Now his emotions and gratitude burst forth in praise.

Ein Karim (the modern name of the village of John's parents) is only about ten miles from Jerusalem. Hence today buses leave the Old City regularly to go there. Visitors can see the imposing Hadassah Hospital with its famous Chagall windows. Ein Karim is mostly Moslem today. There are a few Christian institutions: an orphanage and the convent of the Sisters of Sion, in whose garden their founder, Fr. Alphonse Ratisbon, is buried. The two Catholic churches are associated with the life of John the Baptist. One is built over the reputed home of John's parents. The other marks the site of the Visitation, half a kilometer away. There is also a cave to which Elizabeth is said to have fled to hide her baby boy from Herod. This king had ordered that all male children under two years of age in Bethlehem and the surrounding area be slaughtered (cf. Mt 2:16-18). Ein Karim is not very far from Bethlehem.

The infancy narrative of Luke's Gospel is understood by scholars as a summary and prediction of Jesus' later life, his persecution by that other Herod and the fulfillment of dire prophecies. Luke also saw in the events of Jesus' early life a prediction of the martyrdom of the Mystical Body of Christ, the Church which he records in his "second gospel," the Acts of the Apostles. The application for today is that glory and persecution are commingled in every life and in the Church as well. We must be prepared to accept either. When we are asked the reason for our hope, we should have our answers ready.

John the Baptist was the forerunner of Jesus. He was born a few months before Jesus. They must have been playmates and "soulmates" because the Holy Family came up to Jerusalem for feasts and visited their cousins. Zechariah moreover prophesied, *"And you, child, will be called prophet of the Most High, for you will go before the Lord to prepare his ways."* John appeared near the Jordan thirty years later. He preached the baptism of repentance and announced the coming of Jesus the Savior. Quoting Isaiah, John proclaimed, "Make straight the path of the Lord."

December 24
The Vigil of Christmas, A, B, C

Is 62:1-5; Acts 13:16-17, 22-25; Mt 1:1-25 (long) or 1:18-25 (short)

Matthew's Gospel today is a repeat of texts used late in Advent. The "long form" begins with the genealogy of Jesus. We are familiar with genealogies because of the current emphasis on returning to our "roots." We do this by tracing our ancestors with such means as parish sacramental registers and immigration records at Ellis Island. Matthew traces the ancestors of Jesus in a contrived and artificial way: three sets of fourteen persons, from Abraham to Jesus. Why does he bother? These are the reasons:

First, the writer wanted to show that Jesus was truly a descendant of Abraham and, therefore, a genuine Jew. Jesus is also a descendant of David, and therefore, of the royal family. The title king of the Jews would be nailed thirty-three years later to his cross. God was fulfilling his promise to keep the house of David in power forever through Jesus. Therefore, Paul quotes the prophet in today's second reading, *"I have found David, son of Jesse, a man after my own heart;... From this man's descendants God, according to his promise, has brought to Israel a savior, Jesus."*

Second, the genealogy underscores the humanity of Jesus. He was truly human, not a phantom as the ancient heresy of Docetism held. In the early Church, some Christians did not accept the Incarnation and much less the crucifixion of God-made-man. They asserted that Jesus was a temporarily assumed appearance or a spiritual body. They did not understand, as the sacred writer put it, that he was like us in all things but sin (cf. Heb 4:15).

If we celebrate Christmas mostly with fun and games, except for a brief Mass in church, this holy season might pass us by. We may fail to properly wonder about the meaning of that one life lived two thousand years ago, as well as the meaning of all human life. As we celebrate the birth of Jesus, it is appropriate to commit ourselves to the preservation of life in the womb.

How astounding to learn that abortion is now a multi-million dollar industry, generating over five hundred million dollars annually. The fact that millions of people, even some misguided Catholics, favor abortion-on-demand does not make it right. Morality is not established by vote, nor by passing laws permitting or not permitting something. Morality is established by God's will as expressed in the teachings of Christianity and the Church.

Above all, pray during this season for people's change of heart. Send a contribution to pro-life groups, join a crusade, picket an abortion clinic, write to politicians, telephone government authorities. I know it is confusing when "Christian" theologians endorse a pro-choice position, but Satan never sleeps. Not only is Satan committed to dragging as many souls as possible to hell, but he also seeks to prevent millions of babies from being born. These pre-born babies are killed before they are baptized into God's life.

If we abandon unborn life, we shall see the erosion of the safety and sanctity of all life. Mercy-killing of the elderly, the mentally retarded, the handicapped, the insane, the enemies of the state will follow. Next will be the minorities, peace-protesters, the political party not in power and so forth. You say that couldn't happen here? Just take a look at the history of this twentieth century.

On the eve of Christmas, it may not sound appropriate or pleasant to bring up these moral issues. But we are celebrating in a spiritual way the new life of a special Child. Thus by living our spiritual values, we can help foster love and respect for all human life. We can help build a world where children can grow up in an atmosphere of peace and plenty, of freedom and religion, of stable family life and a happy future.

Christmas
Season

(Midnight) Is 9:1-6;
Ti 2:11-14; Lk 2:1-14;
(Dawn) Is 62:11-12;
Ti 3:4-7; Lk 2:15-20;
(During the Day) Is 52:7-10;
Heb 1:1-6; Jn 1:1-18 (long) or
1:1-5, 9-14 (short)

December 25
Christmas, A, B, C

If you are like me, you probably didn't have time or inclination to read the verses in all your Christmas cards, except, perhaps, the unusual ones from special friends. But if someone you know just had a baby, you no doubt read every line and smiled at the picture of the baby. On the top of the card, there may have been a snapshot of a shriveled-up baby face. Inside would have been the statistics: the child's name, length and weight. And you say to yourself, "Now that's a healthy baby."

Mary and Joseph could not send any birth announcements. They barely found the stable-cave in time. As newcomers to town, they got no coverage in the "Bethlehem Gazette" nor any notice from the town crier. On the other hand, God the Father was certainly proud of his Son (to speak in a human way). The angelic hosts sang with a joy that filled the meadows around Bethlehem.

How do you suppose God the Father would set forth the statistics of his new-born Son, Jesus? Length? From eternity to eternity, his mercy will be endless. His praise goes from pole to pole with one cry. Weight? Why, he is big and strong enough to hold the entire world in his hands. He will be big-shouldered enough to bear a cross that is weighted with the sins of all the world. Yet if you pick up this child and hold him close to you, you will find his yoke easy and his burden light (cf. Mt 11:30).

His name? Isaiah called him *"Wonder-Counselor... Prince of Peace."* He was to be called Immanuel, a name which means "God-is-with-us." The angel told Mary to name the Child Jesus, which means "God-saves" (cf. Lk 1:31). Later he would call himself Son of Man (cf. Mt 8:20; 9:6; 10:23; 11:19, and throughout the gospels). He would also call himself the Good Shepherd (cf. Jn 10:14) and Light of the World (cf. Jn 8:12).

But we can look at him and sum up all his names as Love. In his First Letter John explained that the essential idea of love is *"not that we have loved God, but that he loved us and sent his Son as expiation for our sins."*

No doubt the first visitors to arrive at the stable looked at Jesus, then at Mary and Joseph. Not knowing the divine origin of the Child, they would have asked themselves the usual questions and made the age-old comments. "Who does the Baby favor?" "He's got his mother's eyes." "But he's got his father's mouth and chin."

And Joseph and Mary kept the truth locked in their hearts. They knew that all of Jesus' characteristics and genes could only have come from his mother. Yet in a deeper theological sense, he resembled all of human-kind. He was like us in all things but sin (cf. Heb. 4:15).

The theology of Christmas reminds us that we refer to Jesus often as the Word-of-God-made-flesh. The expression, "word of the Lord," appears 241 times in the

Bible. Most of the time "word of the Lord" opens a prophetic statement, as "The word of the Lord came down
to Jeremiah the prophet." In Hebrew "prophet" comes
from a term which means "mouthpiece," by whom God
was speaking to his people.

Two thousand years ago God spoke his final, full
message when the world was in readiness. God spoke
about himself actually, his self-revelation, a self-
disclosure, in the person of Jesus Christ. In the fullness
of time, God defined himself in the way he wants always
to be known: Love enfleshed, omnipotent power in the
baby fist of a Child, eternal wisdom in the babbling and
gurgling of a babe.

Come, let us adore him and recognize divinity in a
Baby, the Godhead wrapped in swaddling clothes. Ponder the Almighty dependent upon Joseph and Mary for
warmth and protection, the Author of Life kept alive at
the breast of a teenaged mother.

(I take this opportunity to wish you a blessed holiday season. May you discover the wonder of a God who
confined himself to a stable-cave so as to reveal himself
in his essential meaning as Love.)

Sunday in the Octave of Christmas, *Holy Family, A B C*

Sir 3:2-6, 12-14; Col 3:12-21;
(A) Mt 2:13-15, 19-23;
(B) Lk 2:22-40 or 2:22, 39-40;
(C) Lk 2:41-52

Even though Advent, celebrated in somber purple, seems so different from the shining white and gold of the Christmas cycle, they resemble each other thematically. Advent presented the prophecies of the Jewish Testament about Jesus, the prophetic figure of John the Baptist, the conception and birth of Jesus. These elements lead us to see Jesus as the focus and meaning of human history. The Christmas cycle presents the Holy Family as the focus and meaning of individual, personal history. Every believing family can identify with the problems of the Holy Family and apply the answers they found.

The first two readings prepare us for the Gospel. Sirach presents that aspect of wisdom which includes filial reverence. His somewhat naturalistic approach generates the reward promised in the fourth commandment, "so that you will be long-lived in the land God gives you" (Exodus 20:12). Paul reminds the Colossians of the loving obligations of each member of a family, even the slaves.

The Gospel presents Joseph once more, according to Matthew's approach, taking protective leadership over the lives of Jesus and Mary on the flight to Egypt. Matthew shows the "Jewishness" of Jesus. He goes down into Egypt, as did Abraham, Sarah and the family of Jacob. There is considerable early Christian documentation of legends, feasts and writings, despite some mythical material, which underscore the historicity of the flight into Egypt. Some stories are fanciful, but all are charming. Palm trees bend over to deliver their dates to feed the family. Boat-men on the Nile offer to ferry them south to Upper Egypt; there was a well-known Jewish enclave at Syene at the first cataract. In another place, a spring gushes to the surface to refresh the three and provide an opportunity for Mary to wash Jesus' clothes.

Several towns claim that the Holy Family spent the night there, at least in a cave at the outskirts of the village. The Jewish quarters of Egyptian towns would provide a ready sanctuary. The Holy Family may have passed from one to the other.

Today's itinerary would not differ much from that of Jesus, Mary and Joseph. They traveled from Judea towards the Mediterranean coast, through the Gaza strip, towards the Nile Delta. They turned south before Alexandria (although many Jews resided there), then went into Heliopolis and Gizeh (Cairo today). They would have gone south up the Nile. One can hardly substantiate the route of an insignificant couple 2,000 years ago. On the other hand, there is no reason to assume any other route.

The apocryphal ("unsubstantiated") tales of the flight remain constant up to today. Coptic Christians, in particular, maintain continuous traditions about the rest stops of the Holy Family. For example, at Matarieh near Heliopolis (City of the Sun), they rested under a sycamore where Jesus brought forth a spring. Nearby was a temple with 365 idols, one for each day of the year. When the Holy Family took shelter within for the night, all the idols crumbled into pieces in the presence of the true God.

Other kinds of testimony to the flight have come down to us as written sermons, indulgences for visiting pilgrim sites, calendars with such feasts and so on. I visited the ancient Coptic Church of St. Sergius in Old Cairo. A stairway through the main floor leads down to a cave and a pool of water. The Holy Family is said to have stayed there for some time. The cave is under water when the Nile is in flood. This church was erected in the fourth or fifth century.

The value of this feast of the Holy Family lies not in showing that Jesus the Messiah is the fulfillment of a Jewish destiny—at least for us in the twentieth century. Instead, we are to listen to the call of heaven. Joseph listened and learned to leave the familiar and comfortable. We, too, may set out on risky ventures. We trust our heavenly Father to see us through our once and future problems. We look to the time after our wearisome journeys when we return home to heaven.

Joseph and Mary represent all parents. Note how the angel fanfares were silent, their songs stilled. The astrologers were no longer present to confirm their special destiny. The couple could look forward now only to fear, worry, pain, drudgery and the unexpected. All families have their ups and downs.

Mary was pregnant before marriage with a divine Child, miraculously conceived and born without violation of her virginity. Yet she could tell no one—and who would believe her? Her husband, called a just man (cf. Mt 1:19), felt at a loss as to how to educate the boy. But

Mary and Joseph simply took one day at a time and never stopped loving and reflecting. For the rest of their lives, the couple relied on faith and trust, joined to hope, in the performance of the basic, down-to-earth, family chores. They determined to do the ordinary tasks extraordinarily well. In prayer they found strength and solace. Not even the threat of Herod's assassins could dry up their confidence.

Is this not the history of us all? Christians are the family of God. We, too, must find the same answers to life's problems as Jesus, Mary and Joseph. We can: take a day at a time, never stop loving, reflect in hope, find importance in pedestrian obligations, grow in courage through prayer. Jesus and his parents have gone before us to be our example and to sanctify our humanity.

DECEMBER 26-31

December 26
Stephen, Protomartyr

Acts 6:8-10, 7:54-59;
Mt 10:17-22

The title of "protomartyr" is awarded to St. Stephen in the calendar of saints. The term "martyr" implies suffering and even death, but from its Greek root, it also denotes "witness." Yet every saint gives witness to Christ, whether by life or by death. Every saint seems to have undergone suffering in following the way of Jesus. We use the word "protomartyr" of Stephen in the sense of "prototype." That is, he is the model or pattern by which we recognize the original.

Stephen fills the bill very well, indeed. He was a member of the Jerusalem community right from the beginning. Stephen was a deacon, a word—also from the Greek—which means "one who serves." Deacons today generally perform liturgical roles. Originally, they distributed the community's surplus food, clothing and donations to the poor, the orphans, widows and the unemployed. They exercised this loving ministry, as the Bible puts it, to free the apostles for preaching and teaching the Gospel (cf. Acts 6:1-7).

Deacons even then must have been empowered to teach and preach. So it was with Stephen. He debated the Hellenized Jews. These Jews were Roman citizens by virtue of having been born in towns or regions which had been granted Roman citizenship. They likewise were probably under the influence of Greek philosophy and culture. As today's Gospel reads, Stephen did not have to be anxious about what to say because it will be *"the Spirit of your Father speaking in you."* Therefore Stephen bested his adversaries in dialogue which enraged them.

Stephen's mastery of Greek is implied. First of all, his name, which means "crown"—such as worn by winning athletes—indicates his non-Palestinian origin. Secondly, the first lines of chapter 6 state that the deacons were chosen precisely to care for Greek-speaking widows, who believed they were being neglected in favor of the Hebrew-speaking widows.

The most important message of today's feast lies in the likeness between the crucifixion of Jesus and martyrdom of Stephen. Stephen was dragged outside the city, just as Jesus was. In ancient days, cities were held to be sacred and no blood was supposed to be spilled inside the walls. Verse 60 of chapter 7 (which is not in today's text) reports the dying words of Stephen, "Lord, hold not this sin against them," which parallels Jesus' own words, "Father, forgive them. They do not know what they are doing" (cf. Lk 23:34).

On the cross the Master cried out, *"Into your hands I commend my spirit"* (Lk 23:46). Stephen is recorded as saying, *"Lord Jesus, receive my spirit"* (Acts 7:59). This phrase is derived from the psalm taught to Hebrew children as a night prayer. It is still used by the Church as part of Compline, the Night Prayer of the liturgy.

St. Luke, the writer of Acts, obviously took pains to show the parallel between the death of the physical person of Christ and the martyrdom taking place in the Mystical Body of Christ. Indeed, Acts is the continuation of Luke's Gospel, that is, the physical life of Jesus continues in the life of the Church.

The footnote to this passage typically generates the same comment from all writers. We never know the consequences of giving witness to our faith. Stephen's murderers laid their cloaks at the feet of a young man named Saul probably so that they would have a freer arm to stone Stephen. One of the gates of the Old City of Jerusalem is still called St. Stephen's Gate. It is also called Lion's Gate from the decorative sculpture flanking the entrance, as well as the Sheep Gate, near which even today sheep and goats are bought and sold. There is the remains of a quarry just outside the gate from which Stephen's killers took the huge rocks that became their weapons.

So Saul, soon to become Paul, must have stood there wondering about the sway the dead Jesus had over his disciples. Stephen was willing to challenge Jewish leaders, then die for his faith. What Paul did not yet know was that Jesus was alive in glory. That thought which spurred Stephen must be our motive too.

December 27
John, Apostle and Evangelist

1 Jn 1:1-4;
Jn 20:2-8

After many years of re-reading John's three short letters, I have learned that they are profound, basic and deeply theological. Today's text, the beginning of the first letter, purports to be the writer's eyewitness account of the Master. What we have heard, seen, looked upon and touched, claims John, we *"testify to it."* The invisible Godhead became the source of visible life for us. The apostle wants to share that life as the bottom line of his proclamation. His letters do not add new material to the theology of the fourth Gospel. They simply isolate statements about love that sum up Jesus' teaching.

The Gospel today indicates a very significant way of giving witness: by observation, investigation and subsequent declaration. It may be surprising to read about the resurrection a few days after Christmas. But Easter is the reverse side of the coin of the Nativity. During this season, we mark the true humanity of Christ. During Holy Week, we celebrate his death and divine rising to glory. In God's plan of salvation, each event includes the others.

The resurrection scenes have variations in the gospels. In today's text, Mary Magdalene hastened to tell Peter and John that Jesus' body was not in the tomb, implying from her statements that the corpse was stolen. The tomb was on the other side of the Old City from the Cenacle where it is said that the apostles were staying. Walking distance is about twenty minutes at a fast pace. As might be expected of a younger man, John outran Peter in their race for the tomb. Yet John did not enter, but merely peered inside to see the shroud. Either John waited for Peter out of respect for him, or because he was naturally fearful in the presence of such a mystery.

Nothing in the gospels is written casually. Each phrase and sentence has some meaning and purpose, which the Fathers of the Church are quick to exploit. John, the younger apostle, paradoxically represents Judaism. Although an older religion than Christianity, Judaism did not have the mature experience of Christ and his meaning, particularly his arcane prophecies about his resurrection. On the other hand, Peter, soon to be the vicar of Christ, is the man of mature faith, to whom Jesus would say, "When you have been changed, go and strengthen your brothers" (Lk 22:32). Therefore, in the light of the future life of the young Church, Peter's testimony looms larger, especially because he denied Christ and ran away from the crucifixion scene. John the beloved, on the other hand, stayed near Jesus and Mary.

It is not that love, symbolized by John, is less than the faith typified by Peter. It is simply that the point of the Gospel is to give witness to an event, even describing homely details about the shroud and head wrappings. Thus investigation and attestation is another important means of giving witness to our faith.

Although written and spoken testimonies are necessary to establish the contents of faith, it is the application of faith that is the most persuasive. The testimony of a life well-lived in love somehow touches others more effectively than all the written and verbal statements. The proof of faith is acting it out in practical ways within the believing community. As the first reading puts it, *"Our fellowship is with the Father and with his Son, Jesus Christ."*

December 28
The Holy Innocents

1 Jn 1:1-5—2:2;
Mt 2:13-18

Spiritual masters often tell us to prepare for combat when we come to serve God. The slaughter by Herod of these guiltless children under two years of age—*infantes,* which means "unable to speak"—is only one of the discordant notes in the song of Christmas. For Mary and Joseph, there had been no room at the inn after the difficult journey from Nazareth. At the words of Simeon, a sword of sorrow had pierced Mary's heart (cf. Lk 2:35). There was a hazardous journey into Egypt and a long exile. And there was the slaughter of the innocent children, who were not even aware of the combat around them.

The promises of their baby life were snuffed out by the mad rage of a demented king. The hopes of their parents were also extinguished. On the surface, it seems cruel of God to "use" the children as a diversion to distract the soldiers from the real event taking place—the escape of Jesus with his parents. It is up to God to choose the events of history through which he will bring that history to its proper destiny. Just as the circumcision of Jesus, his first "bloodshed" symbolizes his future passion and crucifixion, say the ancient Church writers, so the Innocents symbolize the thousands of martyrs who were to shed their blood over the centuries. The actual number of children is uncertain. It probably lies between six and thirty, not the thousands sometimes depicted in art. Bethlehem and its locality did not have a large population. Children two and under would surely have been few. In any case, the Innocents do not fall into the usual categories of Christian heroes and heroines. They did not prepare for combat because they did not "come" to the service of God; they were drafted. They were certainly not aware of what was happening to them except for the pain of their hopefully swift death.

It may be helpful to speculate about the children themselves. Perhaps they were, at least in some cases, saved from the very loss of their souls. They might have grown up to become criminals or sinners or those who shouted, "Crucify him!" The Church has always honored the Innocents as saints, so we assume these sinless boys, divested of the impediment of earthbound and corporeal existence, would have been directly illuminated by God. Thus they would have achieved their full human potential, as well as the enjoyment of the Beatific Vision. Tragic as was their earthly loss, their heavenly gain was the greater. This is the bottom line and the long-range view. The fact that there is no mention of their massacre in contemporary documents does not lead us to the conclusion that their story is fabricated. Herod was guilty of even more startling murders. As a

puppet king endorsed by the Roman emperor, he believed himself beyond the reach of ordinary law. He put
to death his own wife and children, because he thought
they were threats to his throne. As he lay dying, he realized that the Jewish populace would rejoice at his
demise, especially because he was not Jewish, but Id-
umean. Therefore, Herod ordered that many prominent
Jews be put to death indiscriminately, so that voices of
mourning might be heard throughout Judea when he
himself died.

The first reading from John's first letter points out,
"The blood of his Son Jesus cleanses us from all sin."
Therefore, in view of the future merits of Jesus, the Innocents were freed most surely from original sin in their
baptism of blood. In addition, because they had been
circumcised according to the covenant with Abraham,
this for the Jews was equivalent to baptism, as St. Thomas wrote many centuries ago. Thus the Innocents' title
to heaven's glory was manifold.

One last thought. The Holy Innocents might well be
considered the patron saints of all who are dedicated to
the pro-life movement. Pro-life workers labor against the
evil of abortion as well as the evil of permitting the death
of handicapped infants through the withholding of sustenance and ordinary life support systems.

When you enter into spiritual combat with Satan, be
prepared for suffering. You may get a sword thrust into
your own heart, the sword of frustration and loneliness.
You may even suffer the treachery of those who should
love you most. You may see your ideals slaughtered by
the words and actions of those around you. But Jesus
said, "Take courage, I have overcome the world" (Jn
16:33).

December 29—Fifth Day
in the Octave of Christmas

1 Jn 2:3-11;
Lk 2:22-35

The feast of our Lord's Presentation in the Temple and (formerly) Mary's Purification are celebrated in the Church's liturgical calendar on February 2. According to Jewish law, this is the proper lapse of time. But the text is inserted soon after Christmas, so that we can continue reading Luke's infancy narrative in its proper order. Jesus had already been circumcised on the eighth day, undoubtedly in Bethlehem. On that occasion, he was given his name of Jesus. Circumcision is the ritual that inserted a boy into the covenant of Abraham and the Jewish nation officially. In fact, January 1 was formerly called the feast of the Circumcision of our Lord. Later a first-born son would be "presented" to God in the Temple (when the child was able to travel). At that time, he was ritually "sacrificed" to God, but his parents redeemed or "bought him back" with an alternate sacrifice. In the case of the poor, like Mary and Joseph, the sacrifice was only two birds, turtle doves or pigeons. As was the custom among ancient peoples who sacrificed to their deities, all the sacrificed animals were later sold in Jerusalem meat markets. This greatly contributed to the support of the priests and the liturgy.

It is clearly stated in both Matthew and Luke that Jesus was the first-born of Mary. This, unfortunately, has led some Christians to infer that Mary had other children. This error is against all tradition. The first-born male had special significance as belonging to God, just as the first-born animal or first fruits of the harvest.

The mother was "purified" during the presentation of her child. That is, the issue of blood after childbirth had already stopped. In ancient days, it was often thought that blood was the carrier of human life. Hence the loss of blood made one ritually impure. There is similarly at a Catholic baptism the "churching" of the mother. Formerly, this was delayed for about one month, because often the mother was too weak to attend the baptism of her newly-born child. She did not even attend church until she was formally "churched." Because of the high rate of infant mortality, even in the recent past, the godmother took the child for baptism as soon as possible.

Of course, Jesus did not have to be offered to God nor Mary, the immaculate one, "purified." Yet they submitted to the Law for our sake and to give the example of obedience. Simeon was the holy or "just" man who took Jesus into his arms to bless the Holy One. Then Simeon received a divine blessing himself as he recognized the *"consolation of Israel."* Simeon was like an old watchman at the Temple, pacing the courtyards, walking through the extensive porticoes, scrutinizing every new face to discern whether the *"consolation"* had appeared. Imagine him peering over the parapet on one day, then dancing with the Torah, as the old men did on the feasts. Some other day he would be poring over the sacred texts, always praying to God. Judaism is a very positive and joyful religious tradition. The scenes just described above are possibly more typical of devout Jews than of the scribes and Pharisees who were Jesus' antagonists in the gospels. The Holy Spirit is mentioned twice with respect to Simeon: he would not see death before he saw the Messiah and he was inspired to enter the Temple precincts just when the Holy Family appeared there. He was cast in the role of prophet by that same Spirit: the child would become a sign of contradiction for Israelites. They would *"rise"* or *"fall"* according to whether they accepted the Anointed, that is, the Messiah.

As we perceive the action of the Spirit in Simeon's life, we should apply the lesson to ourselves. Time has no reference to God, who is eternal. But he is always "on time" and acts in a timely way. God does not disappoint those who expect him in patience and long-suffering, like Simeon.

December 30—Sixth Day in the Octave of Christmas

1 Jn 2:12-17;
Lk 2:36-40

Senior citizens and their significant role in human affairs certainly receive their applause in Luke 2. First, Simeon is shown as a *"righteous and devout"* man, who waited until his final days on earth to see the Messiah. Then Anna enters the scene and is similarly praised for her service, fasting and prayer. She was widowed after only seven years of marriage. Computing her age at the time of her marriage at about sixteen and, as the Gospel puts it, *"as a widow until she was eighty-four,"* she would have been serving the Temple for well over half a century. The complicated rituals required special vestments, which had to be sewn, mended and washed. I am sure there were other chores of cleanliness in the inner rooms of the Temple.

Even though she would have been excused because of her age, Anna gave herself to constant prayer and fasting. Nowhere else in the Christian Testament do we read of another *"prophetess,"* a lady "mouthpiece" or spokeswoman of the Lord. She must already have established a reputation for "speaking up" for her beliefs and values. She had actually witnessed the building of the second Temple (Herod's Temple) upon the remains of the modest Temple built by Zerrubbabel after the Exile. (Modern Jews do not recognize Zerrubbabel's construction as a true "Second Temple.")

We can learn from Anna that knowing the mind of God—to the degree it is possible—is not an easy or quick task. It takes years of prayer and fasting joined with practical service and lowly work—before one becomes believable as God's mouthpiece. We ought not boast of our insights in prayer and easy communion with God. We don't want to act as if we had the "inside track" with God or are special friends of the Lord. So often we hear people say that they are correct in their viewpoints and decisions because they "prayed over it." Going into a church, sometimes with our minds made up and talking something over with God, does not constitute a special inspiration and a divinely communicated decision. This can be a manipulation of self, of others and especially of those in authority. On the other hand, a decision without prayer would also be self-serving and possibly a self-deception.

Note how after seeing the Christ Child Anna did not allow her insight to remain fallow. She *"spoke about the child to all who were awaiting the redemption of Jerusalem."* Thus her service was not only for Temple worship, but also to other people. Anna symbolizes the true believer by her prayer, her service and her dissemination of the Good News of Jesus.

As we read the close of today's Gospel, we discover one of the most thrilling texts of Luke. *"The child grew and became strong, filled with wisdom; and the favor of God was upon him."* Later in the same chapter, verse 52, Luke repeats this idea. "Jesus, for his part, progressed steadily in wisdom and age and grace before God and man." What marvelous words. When the Second Person was enfleshed, he had to learn human ways by practical experience. He had to make "progress" just as the rest of us must grow, change and learn new ways. Thus he, too, had the adolescent growth spurt. He had the natural satisfaction of feeling his muscles develop and the perspiration pour off his young body as he played and worked in the hot sun. He was like us in all things but sin (cf. Heb 4:15).

As a man born of woman, he grew in grace, that is, the favor of God. He has gone before us to show by his one life the meaning of all life, especially how to love the eternal God and Father of us all.

December 31—Seventh Day in the Octave of Christmas

1 Jn 2:18-21;
Jn 1:1-18

When we read this Gospel, which is the prologue to St. John's Gospel, we are at once struck by several points. *"In the beginning"* is a repetition of the opening words of the first book of the Bible, Genesis: "In the beginning God made the heavens and the earth." It is as if John decided to start all over again and place the "new creation" into its proper context. This prologue is actually the creation story retold with profound Trinitarian theology. *"All things came to be through him"*—the Second Person, the Word of God. *"Without him nothing came to be."* God spoke the words of creation, *"Let there be."* He actually spoke just one Word, his Word, his perfect expression of himself. Notice that the text is divided, not into paragraphs, but into apparent quotations with commentary in between. The indented sections, as scholars point out, are evidently parts of an ancient Christian hymn, which John incorporated into his Gospel.

Just as God first separated the light from the darkness and then created the luminaries in the sky, so John emphasizes that Jesus is the light that overcomes the darkness of error and sin. Darkness always symbolizes the power of evil, the night which masks the deeds of sin and the confusion of ignorance. Through Jesus *"was life and this life was the light of the human race."*

We see the continuing necessity of the first Christians to stress that the popular John the Baptist was merely the forerunner of Jesus. He came *"to testify to the light.... He was not the light.... The true light, which enlightens everyone, was coming into the world."*

It is noteworthy that John did not put down the law of Moses. In fact, he said that *"the law was given through Moses."* Jesus himself said he came not to abolish the law, but to fulfill it. Yet the New Testament gives a higher mandate through love.

It is helpful, as we read the rest of John's Gospel, to see that he is profoundly "theological." However, each evangelist has his own theological strengths and emphases. In John, Jesus is more "spiritual" in the sense that his divinity is more evident. It is not that the humanity of Jesus is less important, but the believer is asked to look beyond the visible event to its ultimate meaning— as in the Prologue itself. In John's Gospel, Mary seems to have great importance in the public life and death of Jesus. No doubt, this is because John was assigned by Christ from the cross to care for her (cf. Jn 19:27).

Today's Gospel is reminiscent of the overture to an opera. The overture establishes the melodies of the songs that will appear in the opera itself. Thus John establishes the themes of his Gospel: the divinity of Jesus, our incorporation into Christ *("What came to be through him")*, light battling the forces of evil darkness, rejection by *"his own,"* Jesus' glory shining through his works and love as the enduring value. These ideas are golden threads in John's tapestry.

Some of the passages require meditation to be applied. *"But to those who did accept him he gave the power to become children of God."* Only Jesus knows the Father and the way to the Father. To be "in grace" means to share in the divine life of the Trinity. *"And the Word became flesh and made his dwelling among us."* Literally this *"dwelling"* means he "pitched his tent" among us. This recalls the ark of the covenant in the tabernacle or tent that traveled with the Jews on Exodus. The Word remains in our midst in various ways: in the Bible, the believing community, the Eucharist. Yet even a tent is transitory, so the Lord accompanies us as we move to his kingdom and towards the end of the world, *"grace in place of grace."* Who can begin to enumerate God's wonders during salvation history and his mercies to us as individuals? What an uplifting daily chore to count one's blessings. *"We saw his glory."* John captures the Jewish concept of the *shekinah.* In the Old Testament, the glory of God was in cloud, fire and smoke. In the New Testament, God's glory is in the power of the Eucharist that remains in our church tabernacles.

January 1
Octave of Christmas

Solemnity of Mary,
Mother of God, A, B, C

Num 6:22-27;
Gal 4:4-7; Lk 2:16-21

Every feast of Mary belongs to Jesus, because Mary lived for him and took her meaning from Jesus. In a marvelous exchange, Mary is the point of access to the human world for Jesus and Jesus is the point of access to the divine world for Mary. Therefore, today is the "Mother's Day" of the Church. We celebrate Mary's physical motherhood of Jesus and her spiritual motherhood of the Church.

Because this is also a feast of Jesus—a woman is not called "mother" until she has a child—we celebrate both the humanity and humanness Jesus received from Mary. In the same moment we recognize that the whole Church must remain "human," in touch with people's felt needs, sensitive to earthbound problems, a part of every family. Sometimes the Church could seem monolithic, legalistic and hierarchical. But the Church is people and all of its members are God's family, the Body of Christ.

Paul's letter to the Church in Galatia sets the theology: Jesus is *"born of a woman"* (4:4). This is the only text of all Paul's letters where Jesus' mother is mentioned, even though not by name. The first reading from Numbers is the blessing given to Jewish worshipers by the high priest. We see that the stern visage of God in the Jewish Testament is softened by the words of this text. It is almost as if the humanness God would express in Christ had begun to break through. *"The Lord let his face shine upon you, and be gracious to you! The Lord look upon you kindly and give you peace."*

God is "one of our kind" in Jesus through Mary. As the Father's adopted children, we have gained the title and right to heaven. We reach fulfillment if we enter into the mystery of Jesus and mold our humanity after the model of his. We begin at the beginning, his conception and birth from Mary. To give birth is a single, transitory event, but "mothering" is lifelong. Mary directed his human and social growth. Jesus learned from her how to say "please" and "thank you." Mary taught Jesus how to use correct grammar and pronounce his baby words right. Jesus learned from his mother how to help with his share of chores and to play childhood games with simple skills. Mary cared for his cuts and bruises and taught him his first prayers to his heavenly Father. Luke's story about his being found in the Temple concludes that Jesus grew in age, wisdom and grace (cf. Lk 2:52), that is, chronologically, humanly and spiritually.

These experiences prepared Jesus to express his feelings and emotions in his adult life, which he did very well. He allowed the fallen woman to bathe his feet with her tears (cf. Lk 7:38). He drove the money-changers from the Temple in anger (cf. Mt 21:12). He wept over Jerusalem, which was to fall (cf. Lk 19:41) and so forth. Thus we learn not to fear. We learn not to suppress our emotions of anger, hate, love, tenderness, pity. We learn acceptance of others with all their faults and failures. As in the case of Jesus, however, our emotions should be guided by reason. Those emotions, then, will lead to reasonable and proportionate actions. Sometimes Jesus was direct and abrasive in his corrections, as with the scribes and Pharisees. He willed to hurt their feelings, even to outrage them, for the good of their souls. He could call his vicar, St. Peter, a "satan," when the latter tried to dissuade him from going up to Jerusalem to die (cf. Mt 16:23). We remember how the resurrected Christ dealt with St. Paul who had witnessed the stoning of St. Stephen (cf. Acts 7:58). Paul must have wondered how the dead Jesus could have had such a command over men's hearts. Shortly afterward, on his way to Damascus to harass and arrest Christians, Paul was struck down by the Lord. The gentle words Jesus spoke to Paul were not destructive, but accepting, *"It is hard for you to kick against the goad"* (Acts 26:14). The Lord recognized his confusion as well as his positive qualities of zeal and dedication.

It is important to pray that those who are entrusted with the difficult task of governing may be as affirming as Jesus was with Paul. Pray that we all may exercise the same Jesus-like affirmation towards each other. When was the last time you said outright to your spouse, parents, close relative or friend, "I love you"? How often do you apologize or seek reconciliation with others? How accepting are you of an alcoholic neighbor or relative? Do you affirm that person's positive qualities? Do you put out your hand to strangers, to a fallen teenager, to a young unmarried mother? All of us—even men—need to "mother" others, so as to bring out the Jesus who lives in us all.

On this feast recognize Mary's role in your Christian and human life. Study the lives of Jesus and Mary in the Bible, especially their expression of emotions and you, too, will understand how to be fully human. Jesus once said, "I came that they might have life and have it to the full" (Jn 10:10). As we discover from the gospels, Jesus and Mary are the supreme teachers in the Church. They have already achieved what we have yet to attain: sinlessness, glory and eternal intimacy with the Father.

As a child, influenced by delightful (if sometimes inaccurate) stories, I thought a host of angels surrounded Mary all the time. I thought they baby-sat with Jesus, helped with the household chores and swept up the wood shavings in the carpenter shop. I imagined Mary getting direct advice from an ever-hovering Holy Spirit on how to raise a divine Child. But now I understand that Jesus was "like us in all things but sin" (Heb 4:15). Mary did not escape distress, anxiety and hard work as mother, wife, homemaker and finally widow. All women should look to her as a model that is both realistic and consoling. Learn to express your feelings in a wholesome way. Be as "human" as you can. Make time for others, especially those whom the Lord has given you to love most of all, your natural and spiritual families.

SECOND SUNDAY AFTER CHRISTMAS

Second Sunday after Christmas, A, B, C

Sir 24:1-4, 8-12;
Eph 1:3-6, 15-18;
Jn 1:1-18

The first reading comes from Sirach, a sage who lived and wrote about two hundred years before Christ. He approaches morality more from the standpoint of nature than grace. Nevertheless, he pauses in his writing to wonder at the ineffable wisdom of the Creator. Yet in the last analysis, the Creator cannot be fathomed by the human mind. Sirach personifies Wisdom: *"From the mouth of the Most High I came forth.... Before all ages, in the beginning, he created me, and through all ages I shall not cease to be."* The Second Person was not created, of course, but the Church uses this text as an adjunct to John's Prologue. *"From the mouth of the Most High"* suggests the Word, Christ. *"In the beginning"* is also the opening line of John's Gospel.

The second reading, the letter to the Ephesians, places us in the mind of God and his eternal plan. God *"chose us in him, before the foundation of the world, to be holy and without blemish before him. In love he destined us for adoption to himself through Jesus Christ...."* John has a similar parallel text today: *"What came to be through him was life, and this life was the light of the human race.... But*

*to those who did accept him he gave power to become children
of God."* We are marvelously predestined to be in
Christ—his Body, as Paul also wrote earlier. Only in the
Body, Christ's Church, can we come to understand and
fully become what we are destined to be. We are sanctified and saved through the Church. God continues to
speak his Word in us and through us to others.

As the Word, Eternal Wisdom, is "hidden" behind
the façade of Jesus' humanity, so the mystery of grace is
hidden under our daily actions. Even the smallest events
of our lives contain the mystery of the divine bursting
through them. The keywords here are watchfulness and
openness, getting behind the appearances of the ordinary. Our vigilance and openness are the necessary
preparation to receive gifts from him, especially his wisdom. This is not mere knowledge, although the facts of
revelation are necessary, too. Knowledge is often just the
accumulation of our own ideas. But God gives us wisdom, which by faith is the application of knowledge to
our salvation. It is of no value to know everything if we
believe nothing.

God asks us to wait for him as he visits us through
his inspirations in prayer, an increase of spiritual life in
the sacraments and his words of wisdom contained in
the Bible. Waiting for God is not easy for us today; we
are always in a hurry. We catch a bus, grab a bite, hit the
books, cook in microwave ovens, eat at fast-food restau-
rants, brew instant coffee and see immediate playbacks
during a game of sports. God's thoughts are not like
ours. He does not exist in time, but in eternity and he
carefully "plans" his strategies for the world. God does
not satisfy anyone who is used to instant gratification.
Virtually everything important in human life requires
waiting: paying off the mortgage, getting a college degree, expecting a baby for nine months, making a marriage work.

Imagine the immigrants of the last one hundred years who came to Ellis Island. Not unlike the believer who seeks the harbor of faith in the new and heavenly Jerusalem, they sought a haven in the New World. The immigrants could see New York across the harbor with its promise of security and prosperity. They waited in the shadow of the Statue of Liberty. They were the world's tired, the poor, the huddled masses the poet Emma Lazarus wrote about. Those immigrants were so near and yet so far. They simply had to wait anxiously until they planted their feet on the mainland. So, too, we wait for our personal judgment day and work out our salvation in fear and trembling (cf. Phil 2:12). In every ordinary human experience, a divine mystery may be concealed, if we are open and vigilant.

Remember when you were applying for a job or waiting to be accepted into a school or program? It was natural if you felt a nagging, worrisome tension after you applied. Remember how you reviewed your actions and words? "Did I say the right thing?" "Did I send in the correct forms?" "Did I register the expected information?" Yet the day of judgment is far more important than a job or school. There is not a salary or degree at stake, but the riches and citizenship of heaven. It will not be just a matter of entering a career, factory, or corporation, but of entering the kingdom. It is not just a matter of arriving in "the land of the free and the home of the brave," but of arriving in that grand and heavenly country where "the saints go marchin' in."

Thus it is helpful to be alert to the hidden meanings of our lives. But no one can do our thinking and meditating for us. When you get a cold at this time of year, you can't pay your neighbor or relative to take your vitamins, fruit juice and the cold pills that make you groggy. No one can go to bed for you and drink hot tea laced with honey, lemon and whiskey. Nor can anyone blow your plugged-up nose for you. You've got to do your own reflecting and praying, penance and conversion. No one else can sweep out the dark corners of your soul and make way for God's Eternal Wisdom that underlies the transitory activities of our world.

Epiphany, A, B, C

Is 60:1-6;
Eph 3:2, 3, 5, 6;
Mt 2:1-12

Epiphany in Greek means a "showing" or "manifestation." God has provided many such manifestations, sometimes called "theophanies" or self-disclosures of God. Adam and Eve, Abraham, Moses, the prophets and kings experienced a theophany. A great Trinitarian theophany occurred during the baptism of Jesus at the Jordan, when all three Persons were evident (cf. Mt 3:16-17). Every self-disclosure is risky because there is the possibility of rejection. Even God, in his self-presentation in Jesus, allows his love for us to be rejected.

Matthew's Gospel today continues to illustrate the writer's intention to favor the neophyte Christians who were converts from Judaism. Matthew wrote at a time when the newly converted Christians were being barred from the synagogues as "heretics" to Judaism. They were suddenly cut off from their ethnic roots and left without an anchor in their own country.

Through his Gospel, Matthew is saying, "Do not worry." Jesus is the spiritual heir of Abraham and Moses. Isaiah and the other prophets promised that all nations would come to Mt. Sion and worship; he is for everybody. Whereas the shepherds were Jewish, poor and unsophisticated, the Magi were Gentiles.

Their gifts reveal that they were relatively rich and learned astrologers. This meant that they were educated in literature, religion, medicine and contemporary science. They were not kings, of course. They had no armies nor even a large retinue of servants. But they were, undoubtedly, the advisers of kings. They were surely part of the international community of scholars, who studied all the sacred writings of antiquity: Egyptian, Persian, Babylonian, Greek and Hebrew.

They were likely to have been influenced by the Jewish Testament, which the Jews had brought with them into the Babylonian Captivity five hundred years earlier. Even if there is uncertainty regarding the dating of the lifetime of Daniel, his exploits in Babylon were probably known and his writings recorded. Hence the Magi were alerted to the time and place of the great Savior's birth. In those days, science was mixed with mysticism and astronomy was linked to astrology.

There are two kinds of astrology, predictive and analytical. Predictive astrology claims to foretell the future, which only God knows and the devil may guess about. Predictive astrology is used on people who are not aware that it is false. Analytical astrology, on the other hand, claims merely to outline supposed planetary influences on individuals from the time they achieve independent life outside the womb. Medieval and Renaissance popes sometimes relied on such analytical astrology as quasi-scientific. However no one has ever conclusively proved the validity of planetary influences.

As for the Magi's star, there are a variety of opinions. Several important astronomers, such as Johannes Kepler, tried to offer explanations. He thought the star was the confluence—coming together—of two planets seen converging from the earth as the vantage point. Giotto, a fresco of the Magi hat event was off by udden explosion of a d the Magi. If so, the ong ago disappeared. star, the confluence of on.

this complex story are s. 2) The search for and ones of risk, sometimes re killed. The Magi risked rod's kingdom without reporting the infant king (cf. Mt 2:12). journey, following our star, visions and dreams. It is is more important than discovering and finding. hy? Because God does not res only the struggle. If our journey ends abruptly, suddenly, unexpectedly, it is only is us still "on the go," still seeking and his justice (cf. Mt 6:33).

JANUARY 2-12
or the Weekdays Following Epiphany

January 2

1 Jn 2:22-28;
Jn 1:19-28

We recall that the Advent gospels proclaimed the appearance of John the Baptist in the desert, preaching, baptizing and encountering Christ. Thus it may surprise us to find him again in the Christmas cycle. We read about him often in the prologue to John's Gospel. However, the Christmas cycle takes us beyond the expectations of Advent. The prologue (December 31) shows the Baptist asserting that Jesus *"ranks ahead of me because he existed before me"* (Jn 1:15). The Baptist adds new information, *"I saw the Spirit come down like a dove from the sky and remain upon him"* (Jn 1:32) (January 3). He seems even to allude to Jesus' sacrificial role: *"Behold the Lamb of God"* (Jn 1:36) (January 4). Mark records an "epiphany" when John baptized Jesus: *"You are my beloved Son; with you I am well pleased"* (Mk 1:11) (January 6). John humbly puts himself in second place: *"The one who has the bride is the bridegroom; the best man, who stands and listens for him, rejoices greatly at the bridegroom's voice. So this joy of mine has been made complete. He must increase; I must decrease"* (Jn 3:29-30) (January 12). The Baptist is the bridge between the old dispensation and the new grace of Christ, celebrated in the Christmas Season.

The delegation or "committee of investigation" that pressed John for an answer sought out this new locust-eating, camel-hair-shirted prophet because they were the guardians of the spiritual heritage of Judaism, the arbiters of orthodoxy. But they seemed to think John had an "identity crisis," because he proclaimed what he was not and confined his self-description to a *"voice."* They asked him why he was baptizing if he was not Elijah returned. (At that time, the Jews commonly used purification baths, not only the Essene sect of Qumran.) John denied that he was a prophet of any sort. His questioners got no satisfactory answer.

John evaded the question of why he was baptizing. He proclaimed that another was on his way—*"whose sandal strap I am not worthy to untie"*—who was going to baptize with water and the Spirit (cf. Jn 1:33; Mk 1:8). John's humility was quite overwhelming. Jesus was his younger cousin. They may well have played (and maybe prayed) with each other when Mary and Joseph made the annual pilgrimage to Jerusalem. This would have been possible because Ein Karim, John's hometown, was only a few miles from Jerusalem. Now John places himself beneath the status of the lowliest slave, whose duty it was to remove the footgear from visitors when they entered the house.

John the Baptist's humility was perfectly self-effacing when he said that Jesus must increase while he must decrease (cf. Jn 3:30). This is a perfect thumbnail sketch of our spiritual life and a summation of the process of putting on Christ (cf. Rom 13:14). Our ego, our self-sufficiency, our self-aggrandizement must cede to Jesus' virtues and values, his lifestyle, his prayer life, his living for other people, his obedience unto death. The last is exactly what happened to John. He was murdered not so much because of Salome, the dancing girl, but because he belonged to Jesus and preached his message to Herod.

Even though we would readily admit that we also are unworthy to unstrap the sandal of Jesus, we, nevertheless, are not exempt from walking in his footsteps.

January 3

1 Jn 2:29–3:6;
Jn 1:29-34

The memory and importance of John the Baptist and his impact on the Jews is such that, even if he had not been the precursor of Jesus, his place in the spiritual history of Judaism would have been assured. His memory was still so "alive" half a century after his beheading that there seemed to be some danger he would "upstage" Jesus. Thus all four gospels take care to clarify John's relationship with the Master.

John testified in today's reading that Jesus is the *"Son of God,"* who would baptize with the same Holy Spirit who had descended upon the Lord (cf. John 1:33). Whenever the Spirit appears, we understand that something special is afoot: the Incarnation, the Presentation in the Temple, Jesus' baptism, his Transfiguration, the Last Supper, Pentecost. The Spirit of Jesus now belongs to the whole Church, the Body of Christ. Although the Church hierarchy guides and governs the Church in Jesus' name, every member has the Spirit as prompter and guide.

Each member of the Body of Christ has his or her specific function as Paul wrote in 1 Corinthians. We eat of one bread and drink of one cup in the Eucharist and so are made one body. We are members not only of Christ, but of each other. We owe our service both to Jesus and to the totality of other members. Each person's gift, talent or charism is designed by the Spirit so that, all together, they present the living and active Body of Christ at work in the world.

The Spirit, our primary spiritual director, sanctifies the world by sanctifying individuals. We are the yeast in the dough, the catalyst in the reaction, the pattern for redemption's application to all mankind. A Christian who does not share in the Eucharist or is an ailing member because of personal sin cannot fulfill the proper function and become part of the integral meaning of the whole Body. The loss of an active charism leaves an emptiness in the appearance of Jesus among us. Everyone has value, because each cannot be replaced. Wasting our earthly life and time is both a personal tragedy and a loss to the Mystical Body.

We do not suddenly appear full-blown in our roles of service to the upbuilding of the Body. Steady growth in self-knowledge and divine knowledge is required. Natural skills and personality factors come into play. It is possible to apply a metaphor to John the Baptist: the molding of his life was like the process by which a bottle of champagne is produced. The bottle ferments in a dark cellar or cave for some years; John prepared himself in the desert. An expert comes by at regular intervals to give the bottle a quarter-turn. So John lived as a Nazirite in Spartan asceticism, unseen and unknown to the world. Meanwhile, the champagne slowly increases in sweetness and an effervescence that can explode the bottle if it is mishandled. Thus John grew in strength and inner power.

Champagne is corked under great pressure, which we can liken to John's impatience to begin his ministry of preaching and baptizing. At the right moment, the sparkling wine shoots its cork into the air and is poured into glasses to be drunk. So John erupted into society like a lion roaring in the desert—or a bottle of champagne that was long in the making.

Nothing is so insipid and sickly-tasting as flat champagne. A prophet without the empowering Spirit of the Lord is like flat champagne. The charismatic dimension of the Church becomes visible in our individual gifts and talents, which bring strength and sweetness to the whole Body of Christ. Insofar as we allow ourselves to decrease and Christ to increase, the full image of Jesus will become clear in this world.

January 4

*1 Jn 3:7-10;
Jn 1:35-42*

The gospels for January 4 and 5 describe the call of Andrew and Simon Peter, Philip and Nathanael. There is a small disagreement as to the details of their call. Philip is said to be from Bethsaida, the same town as Andrew and Peter. Yet Andrew and Peter are described as fishermen from Capernaum, which is, however, near Bethsaida. The other evangelists record that the call of the first disciples took place in Galilee, not near the Jordan, where they apparently had been listening to the Baptist.

Leaving the solution of this minor problem to scholars, let us rather look in John's writings at the vocation of the disciples. Andrew and Simon Peter had to stay with Jesus to hear his words. Philip listened to Jesus, then told Nathanael, who also had to hear for himself.

Hearing someone is not quite the same as listening. Listening requires an inner silence and alertness to the meaning behind another's words. We come to know others by listening to their words—what they stand for, what they value and cherish. The disciples must have first been attracted by the calm gravity of Jesus and his authoritative manner of addressing the crowds. But they had to know him before they could fully respond to his call. Their faith in him had to lead them beyond faith to the love, compassion and mercy that were the basis of his ministry. They had to examine his interpersonal relationships, see him retire for prayer in solitude and observe his patience in teaching about the true nature of the Messiah. Finally, they had to witness his willingness to die for his doctrine. They watched Jesus use his natural skills and especially his emotions creatively through forgiveness, sympathy, anger, resoluteness, spiritual joy and love.

Faith without good works does not survive very long. Faith is the stepping stone to love's good works. In fact, even apparent good works themselves are useless without love, as St. Paul points out in his celebrated pericope, 1 Corinthians 13:1-13. How many believers are not lovers. How many keep God's law without enthusiasm. Faith may detach us from this world, but only love can attach us to God's world. Jesus was not content that his disciples would believe him. They had to love him. How else could they come to die for him?

The Church has been reading the first letter of John since Christmas. Love is John's theme, too; he was known as the beloved disciple. He probably wrote his letters before his Gospel; many phrases and ideas appear in both. The great simplicity of the first letter belies its deep theology. Beginning with his own feast on December 27, John touches many topics, but keeps returning to love as the sign of Jesus' presence. He proclaims only what he has seen, heard and touched, that is, eternal life become visible in Jesus. If we do not deny our sinfulness, Jesus will cleanse us in his blood, the offering for the sins of the world. "But whoever keeps his word truly has the love of God made perfect in him" (1 Jn 2:5). Whoever continues in the light loves his brother (cf. 1 Jn 1:7). If anyone loves the world, the Father's love has no place in him, for nothing that the world affords comes from the Father (cf. 1 Jn 2:15-16).

The antichrists are those who left the ranks of Jesus, who deny that he is the Christ—the Anointed. "See what love the Father has bestowed on us in letting us be called children of God" (1 Jn 3:1). "No one whose actions are unholy belongs to God, nor anyone who fails to love his brother" (1 Jn 3:10). "This, remember, is the message you heard from the beginning: we should love one another" (1 Jn 3:11). "That we have passed from death to life we know because we love the brothers. The man who does not love is among the living dead" (1 Jn 3:14). "The way we came to understand love was that he laid down his life for us; we too must lay down our lives for our brothers…. Let us love in deed and in truth and not merely talk about it" (1 Jn 3:16, 18). All these quotations show that John learned the words and lessons of Jesus very well.

January 5

1 Jn 3:11-21;
Jn 1:43-51

When Jesus chose his disciples, their friendship with the Lord began. That friendship was destined to last even after Jesus' Ascension into heaven. Genuine love transcends the barriers of death. At the Last Supper, Jesus told the apostles that he would no longer call them servants but friends (cf. Jn 15:15). In John's continuing emphasis on love, he directs us to transfer our love for Jesus to one another, just as he himself did. *"The way we came to know love was that he laid down his life for us; so we ought to lay down our lives for our brothers."*

It has been said that a person can love only as intensely as he or she is capable of hatred. John cites the case of Cain and Abel in his first letter today. We can presume, then, that Cain was capable of the same intense emotion in a positive direction, all the more because it concerned his brother Abel. Perhaps we can begin to understand why we read so much about those who maintain a love-hate relationship with a spouse, parent or friend. Jesus seems to recognize this when he tells us to pray for our enemies and those who persecute and calumniate us (cf. Mt 5:44). One wit put it this way: Love your enemies; it will drive them crazy. That, of course, is not our motive, but Paul likened such an act to heaping coals of fire on that person's head (cf. Rom 12:20). *"We have passed from death to life because we love our brothers."* In other words, just as Jesus resurrected by the power of that love that led to the sacrifice of the cross, so we first die to our old selves, then rise to new life in Christ. In fact, the life of every believer should reveal Jesus to others. If we examine more closely why non-Catholic sects make so many converts, especially among the young, we would discover it is often because of the love and understanding shown. Doctrine enlightens the intellect, but love moves the will. Our vocation must be to the heroism of love.

Some words of Jesus seem hard and without compromise. "Unless you do penance, you shall likewise perish" (Lk 13:3). "Unless you are born again of water and the Holy Spirit, you shall not enter the kingdom of heaven" (Jn 3:5). *"Unless you eat my flesh and drink my blood, you will not have life in you"* (Jn 6:53). (The last two texts prompted early Christians at the baptism of their children to have the priest dip the tip of his finger in the Precious Blood. He would then touch the baby's tongue. This still happens in some of the Eastern Catholic rites today.)

Christ's supreme mandate, however, is that we love one another. A friend, it has been written, is a gift you give yourself; he or she is an extension of yourself. As a Latin poet wrote, "A friend is the 'other half' of one's soul." The same is true of our friendship with the Lord. As with our close friends, we share intimacy with Jesus.

We take a risk in honest self-disclosure. Jesus does the same with us. He shares his divine secrets with us. He takes a risk that we will reject him through sin. We become his "extension" as he shares his very nature with us through grace.

If a close friend is a gift, then let us receive the gift of Jesus himself, especially in the Eucharist. We can likewise give ourselves to him entirely as the gift he desires to receive from us. Any gift we give him that does not include ourselves is too little.

January 6

1 Jn 5:5-13;
Mk 1:7-11

Immediately after baptizing Jesus, John saw the sky split apart and the Holy Spirit descend upon the Lord. The voice of our heavenly Father proclaimed him to be his *"beloved Son."* Thus the stage was set for Jesus' ministry. The Trinity is the central doctrine of Christianity. Jesus, with whom the Father was *"well pleased,"* was the way to the Father. Only he knew the Father as he is. Many are the Gospel texts which allude to Jesus' anointing by the Spirit. Thus the doctrine of the Trinity was slowly revealed.

The life we have as believers comes from being drawn out of ourselves, as it were, into the love life of the Trinity. Paul says, "I no longer live, but Christ lives within me" (Gal 2:20). It may be more precise to say that we live in Christ and in the Trinity. In John's first letter, the three witnesses to the presence of Jesus' life in us are the Spirit, the water and the blood. This is a profound, but simple theological insight. The Spirit, to whom we ascribe the sanctification of the world, calls us without our having deserved it. He calls us to holiness, sometimes before we are aware of it. This would be the case of infants, whom the community presents to God. We were predestined before all ages to receive this call. Thus life and washing are given through the water of Baptism. This is the sign of our incorporation into the life of Christ and of his Body, the Church. Among the ancients, blood was the carrier or vehicle of life. (It flows through every part of our bodies except in dead cells such as our skin, nails and hair.) The blood of Christ was life-giving to us, because the Church was born out of his side on Calvary. Of course, the Eucharist provides the possibility of our sharing in his Blood. In so doing, we affirm our willingness to shed our own blood as a witness to Jesus' sacrifice.

These three testimonials appear in John the Baptist's life. He saw the Spirit over the Jordan. He did not need Baptism himself, because Jesus freed John from original sin when he was still in Elizabeth's womb (cf. Lk 1:39-56). As for the witness of blood in his own life, John was beheaded for his uncompromising stand on the immorality of King Herod's marriage. Every follower of Christ must reflect on these three witnesses—the Spirit, water and blood—in his or her life.

John the Baptist fell in line behind the earlier prophets of Judaism who fled the cities for the purifying experience of the desert. The self-denial of these prophets included: no fires from cooking and heating, no over-indulgence in eating and drinking, no noises and interruptions to inhibit listening to the voice of God, no gainful employment to distract from prayer. And always there was the burning desire to love God perfectly. Perhaps after a learning experience with the Qumran monks, John may have left to fulfill his own destiny. He was to be a precursor, who would "run ahead" of Jesus to prepare his way. He was as feisty as his father, the priest Zechariah, who argued with Gabriel and was struck dumb for a time (cf. Lk 1:20). John thought he could find God his Father in the desert. He also found

God the Son and God the Holy Spirit as well. The gossips of the hill country, after the extraordinary events surrounding his birth, asked, *"What, then, will this child be?"* (Lk 1:66). Thirty years later they found out. What is most marvelous about John is that he, who came in the spirit and power of Elijah, who attracted a large following and was so aggressively fearless, submitted himself to Jesus: "He must increase while I must decrease" (Jn 3:30). What a role model for us all.

Everyone needs quiet time alone periodically. What a great spiritual help it would be to create "desert space and time" daily for ourselves. We could encounter God, learn to listen, develop a calm peace of soul, prepare to accept suffering (which we all have) and even death (whenever and however it comes) and let Jesus increase in us.

One does not go into such a desert to make a deal with God—so much suffering and penance for so much reward and glory. This is a bankbook spirituality in which sin is a deduction and good deeds compound the interest. The observance of the commandments and precepts is not enough. The mere absence of sin is too little. When we go into the desert to love God perfectly, we will recognize that this is no mirage.

January 7

1 Jn 5:14-21;
Jn 2:1-12

The wedding feast of Cana is one of those texts which is never exhausted. However, commentary can become tedious after reflecting on the unadorned simplicity of the narrative. The Jewish Testament prefigured this mystical scene. The newly-married couple were the unknowing carriers of a profound mystery. Often in Jewish history, God referred to his people as his bride, to his various covenants as marriage contracts and false worship of pagan gods as adultery. We upon whom the final age of this world has come (cf. Heb 1:2) always need to understand the Christian Testament as the flowering and fulfillment of the earlier, ancient symbols. When Jesus appeared at the feast to bless a human marriage by his presence—even though the couple had eyes only for each other—he implicitly canonized the Jewish prefiguration of Christian marriage. Yet Jesus could not say publicly to his followers during his ministry that the analogy of marriage applied to himself in the clear way it referred to Yahweh in the Jewish Testament. This would have outraged the Jews before they had had the opportunity to know and accept him and his total message.

St. Paul points out that marriage symbolizes Christ's love for his Church (cf. Eph 5:23ff.). A groom fulfills the analogy by loving his wife as Christ loved the Church and died for her. The bride should obey her husband as the Church obeys Christ.

John's Gospel is the "mystical Gospel," concealing the mysteries of grace and life in Christ from the uninitiated. Here the mystery is operative on several levels. The Lord of the universe, that Divine Word by whom everything came into being, changed water into wine, a miracle whereby he *revealed his glory.*" Because God does nothing poorly, the Lord provided a superior vintage, a "choice wine." Some Fathers of the Church liken the plain water to Judaism and the time of preparation. The wine represents Christianity which was born of the water of Judaism. The large amount of water changed into wine not only guaranteed the continuation of the party, but also points out the superabundance of the heavenly banquet and the joy that will be ours in the heavenly Jerusalem. Besides the divine level of mystery, we recognize the human dimension. Jesus acted behind the scenes to save the groom embarrassment. How touching was the Lord's human sensitivity. He anticipates his public ministry to show how God willingly enters human life and our personal history to save us. Perhaps the wine may have run out because of the thirsty apostles who had accompanied Jesus. In that case, his mother would have delicately pointed out the unfortunate situation. *"My hour has not come,"* was the Lord's rather abrupt response.

But a mother, especially this mother, knew her Son's heart. All she had to do was mention the problem, confident that her intercessory prayer would be effective. She told the waiters what she tells us, *"Do whatever he tells you."* The Gospel is perennial. Each passage has some universal application; every text is pertinent for all time. Hence Mary continues to direct us to Jesus, to do *"whatever he tells you."* Her influence with Jesus remains effective and she intercedes for us even in small matters.

St. John is sometimes called the Eucharistic evangelist. Jesus promises to give the world his Body to eat and his Blood to drink. This astounding claim was more believable after the miracle of Cana and the multiplication of the loaves and fish.

There must have been considerable bewilderment at the wedding. Imagine the waiters, the steward, the groom. Even though the Master kept a low profile, news of the incident raced through the party. As always, Jesus preferred that people accept his doctrine rather than be impressed by his wonders. But his awestruck disciples *"began to believe in him."* After three years of instruction, the apostles would learn that the signs which would define Jesus' ministry were not water and wine, but water and blood.

January 7
or Monday after Epiphany

1 Jn 3:22—4:6;
Mt 4:12-17, 23-25

St. John's masterful epistle continues its grand themes. Today's text gives the reader a sense of urgency to beware of the followers of error. They are traitors to Christ who deny that he has come to earth in the power of God. He calls them minions of the antichrist, who is already prowling the earth. We typically identify the antichrist as the master of evil who will come at the end of the world to do battle with the forces of good. St. John, on the other hand, declares that the antichrist is already drawing up the battle lines. We do not know whether the author is recording his apocalyptic vision of the future day of doom or simply warning believers to be watchful at all times.

The antichrist speaks the language of the world, which is foreign to the meek and humble Savior described in Isaiah's Suffering Servant Songs (cf. Is 42—53). The antichrist is allied with money, political power, display and arrogance. He uses threatening force to take the heart right out of men and women of good will. Whence shall come the resistance of believers? From their love for one another, John goes on to say, and from their assertion of the truth they have from Jesus Christ.

The antichrist will be the summation of all the pagan gods of ancient and modern times. Their spirit includes: seductive and permissive immorality, condonation of promiscuity and perversions, superstitious beliefs and degrading cults. These were the stock in trade of many ancient religions and the witchcraft of the Middle Ages. All of these are revived today in various forms. The antichrist has never been absent from the minds and hearts of worldlings. As a ploy, the antichrist and his followers also ape genuine religion to seduce the weakminded.

So the voice of John the Baptist echos down the centuries: "Reform your lives. The kingdom of God is at hand" (Mt 3:1). As Jesus went north into the *"Galilee of the Gentiles,"* he manifested himself as a light *"on those dwelling in a land overshadowed by death."* Legislators today bring the shadow of death and ally themselves with the antichrist who legalize perversion, abortion and the arms race for gain. Jesus came to bring us life, not murder. He came to bring truth not superstition. He came to bring food, after which we need to hunger no more, and peace, which this world cannot give.

From the moment of Jesus' obscure birth, there were no apparent prospects for manifesting his importance and influence. As he grew to adulthood until the moment of his seeming failure on the cross, the Master avoided the trappings and display of his adversary, the antichrist. There would be no royal crown for him in Jerusalem, no army at his side to expel the Romans. He would have no treasures to buy the allegiance and homage of others. All of these, of course, were temptations Satan had unleashed at the beginning of Jesus' public life. Political and even ecclesiastical power were alien to his message. He sought to have influence without coercion. The freedom he offered was not the mere absence of servitude, but the assumption of duties to be able to reign with his Father. We can act no differently as his followers. Everyone will be free when no one desires to command, only persuade.

The Church, Christ's Body, in the final apostasy (cf. 2 Thes 2:3), may have its traitors seduced by the antichrist. Some could choose power and wealth instead of humble service and loyalty to the Gospel. The Tradition of the Church has gained momentum for two thousand years and it will rush forward until the end of time. Perhaps its mighty thrust is slowed at times. The vast throng of its adherents may dwindle, or its proud fortresses may be temporarily besieged. But divine Tradition cannot fail as long as the Church holds its steady course and believers hearken to its voice.

Through his Church, Jesus continues to oppose the antichrist. He proclaims the Gospel and heals the ailing. The Body of Christ is perpetually young and vigorous. Simultaneously, it is perpetually old and wise. The world does not yet belong entirely to the antichrist. It never will as long as one believer chooses not to live by the antichrist's philosophy, as long as one Christian refuses to live for pleasure alone, as long as one Catholic falls to his knees, lifts his hands, and prays, "Father in heaven."

January 8 or
Tuesday after Epiphany

1 Jn 4:7-10;
Mk 6:34-44

St. John's letter has this important statement, *"In this is love: not that we have loved God, but that he loved us and sent his Son as expiation for our sins."* The term "love of God," therefore, applies primarily to God's action in us, rather than vice versa.

In today's Gospel, Jesus was followed by a vast crowd, which, far from home and growing hungry, won his pity. Most commentators suggest that Jesus' compassion was for their physical hunger, but a careful reading of the text indicates a deeper truth, a deeper hunger. Jesus pitied them, it says, because they were like sheep without a shepherd. His response to this figure of speech was, *"he began to teach them many things."* The hunger of the crowd was essentially spiritual. They were seeking the truth about the kingdom of God. The lateness of the hour gave Jesus the opportunity to reinforce his teaching with a miracle. He came that we might have life and have it to the full. This scene touches all these dimensions of life: spiritual, physical, social and intellectual.

This Gospel suggests the Eucharist of the Last Supper, because of the characteristic way in which Jesus handled food. Then *"looking up to heaven, he said the blessing, broke the loaves, and gave them to [his] disciples to set before the people."* The parallel gestures are to be found in the synoptic versions of the Last Supper. Further, when the two disciples recognized Jesus in the breaking of the bread at Emmaus (cf. Lk 24:31), it was because he used his characteristic gestures.

This was the fulfillment of other Gospel promises. Jesus said: *"Whoever loves me will keep my word, and my Father will love him, and we will come to him and make our dwelling with him"* (Jn 14:23). Jesus also promised to give fountains of living water so that we would never thirst (cf. Jn 4:13-14). In the words of Jesus, the physical is the point of departure for the spiritual. The social dimension of Jesus' words is implicit here. Today we are aware of the great numbers of men, women and children who are homeless and hungry most of their lives. They are exploited, disenfranchised by their governments and robbed of their dignity and freedom. Sometimes, in fact, in our own neighborhoods, the jobless, the poor and hungry are overlooked. We might share the Eucharist and greetings of peace with the needy. Then we leave Mass and conveniently forget that Christ suffers in them. Even handouts are only momentary help. We need to reverse the course of social ills with the salutary medicine of justice and peace. We may slip a few dollars into a poor man's pocket and make up food baskets for the holidays. But the cry of the poor is a daily petition (cf. Ps 9:13).

When Jesus worked his miracle of multiplication, he did not discriminate between the rich and poor, the smart and ignorant, the sophisticated and naive. He looked at the interior attitudes of the listeners. He valued the people not for what they could do for him, but for what he could do for them. This amazing reversal of the familiar sentiment is precisely the point of St. John's description of love today: *"not that we have loved God, but that he loved us and sent his Son as expiation for our sins."* If sin were eradicated from life, then there soon would be no poor, no homeless, no exploited. When Jesus takes up his residence within us, he makes us more sensitive to the plight of others.

Whether you picture the Divine Indwelling as God in you or you in God, the net result is the same. A bond of unity arises with all other human beings even outside the Mystical Body. This Divine Indwelling provides easy communication and accessibility to one another. Most of all, it causes assimilation to him who dwells within us. We are enabled to develop the virtues and qualities of Jesus himself. Hopefully, all people will gravitate to the truth of the Eucharist, not only as the basis of the Church's social program, but also to win the ultimate freedom—from everlasting death. "Whoever eats my flesh and drinks my blood I will raise up on the last day" (Jn 6:54).

January 9 or
Wednesday after Epiphany

1 Jn 4:11-18;
Mk 6:45-52

One clear implication of *"perfect love"* is our relative, if not absolute, freedom from sin at this particular moment of our lives. Sin impedes our possibility of being perfect as our Father in heaven is perfect (cf. Mt 5:48). Sin is the barrier to easy communication with God, because it puts us on a different "wavelength." When such impediments as pride, covetousness, lust, sloth and excesses disappear, why should we fear the God who is pleased with us? (Cf. Lk 3:22). *"Perfect love drives out fear."* We who follow the way of Jesus become, in fact, more fully alive, that is, more human. Our detractors claim that religion debases mankind and leads to a superstitious dread of God, whose fury we feel the need to placate.

History shows the opposite. The most dedicated Church persons were deeply sensitive to the love of God and his poor. Their "perfect love" did not derive from seeing God directly. St. John writes in his letter today that the Divine Indwelling led them to love their neighbor whom they did not see. *"Fear has to do with punishment,"* John continues, but those who are intimate with God no longer fear punishment. Therefore religion fosters human dignity. Where the values and prohibitions of religion are absent, human dignity suffers. One way for the believer to judge his or her religiosity is to recognize the degree of concern for the suffering. That concern is manifested in face-to-face contact with the needy, the hungry, the sick, the lonely, the poor, the handicapped.

We realize the need for an informed conscience. It is too easy to accept a debased morality which indulges in one's pleasure. We could also feel sorry for the criminal instead of his victims. We could condone immorality or adopt avant-garde viewpoints to appear knowledgeable or become popular. Thankfully, the teaching of the Church and centuries of Christian wisdom provide guidelines for the formation of conscience. Godless humanism is an intellectual disease that makes mankind's own fallible reason and its convenient logic the norm of human activity. Yet without religious conviction, genuine human activity is never complete. (These ideas are beautifully and succinctly summed up in the Vatican

Council II document: *Pastoral Constitution on the Church in the Modern World [Gaudium et Spes].)*

After Jesus fed the five thousand men, plus the women and children, he sent his disciples off in one of their fishing boats. They sailed across the north end of the Sea of Galilee to the area of Bethsaida. This called for rowing about fifteen miles against the wind. Meanwhile, Jesus wanted to be alone to pray. In any case, the journey would probably have been faster on foot. It was almost dawn and the disciples were exhausted from rowing. A squall had raised terrifying waves, which is not unusual for the Sea of Galilee. The wind comes funneling through the mountain passes and unsettles the surface of the sea.

Even the manifestly casual or trivial acts and words of Jesus were never without their divine purpose. He walked over the water and seemed to pass the apostles by without notice. Yet he was certainly aware of their plight. Torn by their fear of drowning and their fear that what they saw was a *doppelganger* (a "double" or "ghost" of a living person), they cried out in terror. Jesus climbed aboard and quieted both their nerves and the sea.

Jesus had his hands full with those disciples. *"Their hearts were hardened."* They didn't catch on to the miracle of the loaves and fish. They couldn't imagine how and why Jesus had walked on the water and stilled the waves. If his own immediate followers did not grasp his intent, how much less the rest of the Jewish population. The disciples had witnessed the great number of cures and exorcisms, but that might have been expected of a prophet, a holy man. Jesus acted in a divine way and performed the works of God, so that gradually the disciples would see the divinity breaking through his humanity. He healed. At Cana he had turned water into wine and his disciples had begun to believe in him (cf. Jn 2:11). He forgave sin (cf. Mk 2:7). Who but God could do that? He acted as the Lord of the Sabbath (cf. Lk 6:5) and so on. Yet the apostles' faith would remain insecure until they had seen the risen Jesus. All that they witnessed now was the preparation.

Jesus acts no differently with us. After we begin to believe in him, he draws us into a deeper faith. He proves his love for us; he shows his providence and divine power in our personal history. His "small miracles" on our behalf are designed to prepare us to believe in the essentials of his teaching and ministry, particularly his resurrection, by which he overcame sin, death and Satan. Without that supreme event and its historical certainty, our religion would be empty and we would be the most unfortunate of all (cf. 1 Cor 15:19). If Jesus has not freed us from sin and death, there is no reason to hope. We would have failed to see his divinity break through into our lives. We would remain fearful. But John reminds us today that *"One who fears is not yet perfect in love."*

January 10 or
Thursday after Epiphany

1 Jn 4:19—5:4;
Lk 4:14-22

Even though few of us will be remembered more than two generations after we die, most of us want to leave some mark of our passage on earth. Perhaps we want our name scratched in wet concrete, our manuscript published or children who bear our name. Movie stars, statesmen, athletes, military heroes, authors and financiers achieve a few moments "in the sun" of applause. But soon they are relegated to the footnotes of history books. The famous contemporaries of Jesus, had they not lived and affected the life of Christ and his Church, would be only a curiosity of the scholars of antiquity and another assignment of history students.

Jesus was born during the reign of Augustus Caesar. At that time, the *imperium* imposed common laws in the Mediterranean area and developed a diverse network of roads. Thus unwittingly the Roman Empire prepared the way for the rapid spread of Christianity. Caesar was declared a god even though the true God had come among us to make it possible for us to share in his Godhead through sanctifying grace. Jesus lived most of his life in obscurity. His intrinsic holiness was hidden by his ordinary existence within a Jewish family in Nazareth. Yet because of him, the land where he lived is now called the "Holy Land." Significant events of his life are marked with liturgical celebrations that eclipse the publicized liturgies of this world: the Olympics, presidential inaugurations, coronations and the Rose Bowl parade.

However, all of this began quite humbly. After the unusual events that marked the birth of Jesus, known only to a few, Jesus did not appear in the public eye until his baptism in the Jordan. He returned, then, to his hometown to preach in the synagogue. His mother and his family probably attended also. The building was rather small, because ancient Nazareth did not exceed five hundred persons in population. *"All in the synagogue looked intently at him."*

The evangelists report different reactions to his claim that the prophecy of Isaiah referred to himself. His "brothers and sisters," evidently "cousins" according to the Aramaic usage, thought he was "beside himself" or "out of his mind" and they wished to lock him up as an embarrassment to the family. The citizens of Nazareth, hearing that he claimed to be the Messiah, tried to throw him off the cliff on which Nazareth is built (cf. Lk 4:24). Yet Luke's text today records without drama that those in the synagogue *"spoke highly of him and were amazed at the gracious words that came from his mouth."* Either the people had a change of heart by the end of the service, or the evangelists recorded differing reactions (cf. Mt 13:54-58; Mk 6:1-6; Lk 4:16-30).

After the many cures and miracles, Jesus' reputation had spread. He thought he could be prudently open in his discourses. Later he reverted to parable and lessened his stress on his messiahship, lest his audience conclude that he intended to start a revolution against Rome. Jesus avoided the limelight, yet he is better known and revered than anyone who ever lived. More books have been written about him than anyone else in history. He has captivated more hearts and commanded deeper allegiance because he rose from the dead and is alive in heaven today.

We who constitute his Mystical Body, grafted like branches into the life-giving vine, share in the messiahship, the work of the Anointed One. Paradoxically, when we let ourselves decrease, we allow Jesus to increase. We can achieve a share in his immortality which is more certain and secure than siring children, building an industrial empire, or writing an armful of best-selling novels. If we have only one life to spend or invest, let us invest it in the work of the kingdom. This work transcends time. Like Jesus, we are called *"to bring glad tidings to the poor. He has sent me to proclaim liberty to captives and recovery of sight to the blind, to let the oppressed go free,and to proclaim a year acceptable to the Lord."*

Jesus chooses us to be his hands to serve the poor and free the captives. We are his head to think through human problems, spread Good News and announce a jubilee of graces from God. We are to be his heart, so he can more visibly love our race as we imitate Jesus' virtues. This is the faith that conquers the world, outlasts fame and fortune and is stored in the everlasting memory of God.

January 11 or
Friday after Epiphany

1 Jn 5:5-13;
Lk 5:12-16

We often read in the gospels that Jesus touched others. This was not like the telephone commercial's invitation to "reach out and touch someone" by placing a long distance call. Jesus' touch was physical. He laid healing hands upon the sick. He picked up the children who flocked to him. He took a dead person by the hand and applied a paste of clay and his own spittle to a blind man's eyes. In today's text, the leper came up and bowed to the earth; he begged Jesus to cure his leprosy. *"Jesus stretched out his hand"*; he touched the man. (Leprosy was a generic term meaning many blemishes and skin eruptions. Thus we are not certain about the nature of his affliction.) By touching the man, Jesus bypassed the Jewish prescription of avoiding contact with lepers.

The implication of Luke's Gospel is more subtle than is immediately obvious. In effecting the cure, Jesus did not appeal in a mediatory role to his heavenly Father. Acting on his own authority as God, he straightforwardly announced, *"I do will it. Be made clean."* He told the man, however, to subject himself to the law and make an offering to the Temple as Moses had commanded. He was probably given a written statement by the priests who certified the healing. This writ was necessary in case anyone objected to the former leper's resumption of his ordinary life in his hometown.

Lepers were excluded from society. They had to warn others of their approach. They could not handle dishes, clothes or tools used by other persons. They could not even draw water from the common drinking sources. Because they could not work with or for others, they depended on alms. Thus when Jesus reached out and touched the leper, he risked contagion as well as ritual impurity. He could have received a sanction in religious law that might also declare Jesus "untouchable."

We may not have the healing touch of the Master's hand, but we, too, have the ability to heal spiritually. We have these opportunities: when a crying child needs his or her tears wiped away, when a friend or spouse is deeply hurt by an affront, when a friend or neighbor is bereaved, when a teenager feels he or she is a failure in school or social life and when a terminally sick patient is alone and fearful. Then our touch, our kiss, our embrace can uplift, heal and soothe troubled spirits. In each of these cases, the hands of Jesus hold our own hands and transmit his touch through us.

Various cultures and nationalities allow for different lengths of "personal space" around themselves. In North Africa and the Near East, two men will be conversing while their noses are only six inches apart. This distance is socially threatening and unacceptable to men in the United States. To cross that invisible boundary suggests either a threat or intimacy. A similar barrier exists with respect to eye contact. Our eyes whisk across the faces of others, but seldom fix on just one person except when we are experiencing extreme emotion, such as anger, affection, or fearful wariness. When strangers approach us on the sidewalk, they may engage our glance at a distance, but typically turn away when they are about ten feet away from us. Few of us find the "courage" to greet strangers and "touch" them with our eyes.

Children are the significant exception to this rule. Even babes in arms will stare at a person close by. We stare back because a baby is not threatening. Jesus told us to become like little children (cf. Mt 18:3). To reach out and touch another with a glance, or a smile, shows our humanness. Of course, we can also be rejected when we display our affection, concern or sympathy. If this hap-

pens when our barriers are down, we feel like we have
been slapped in the face. Our physical perception of
emotional values are reflected in such popular expressions as, "How does that grab you?" and "Dig that
fellow!" and "He can see through you." That is why it
is important to make the liturgical greeting of peace realistic: to shake another's hand firmly, to kiss your
spouse with holy affection, to smile and meet the eyes
of the other person.

Before Jesus could heal, he had to have the sick person's trust and faith. By faith we can wonderfully touch
God in Christ. He does not remain at a distance, nor
make a personal space around him. He so deeply in-
vested himself in our humanity that he retains his human nature forever in heaven.

January 12 or
Saturday after Epiphany

1 Jn 5:14-21;
Jn 3:22-30

At the end of the Christmas Cycle, we return to John
the Baptist and his enclave of disciples near the Jordan
at the edge of the desert. Actually, three groups in that
locality are of interest to us. The monastery of the
Essenes was at Qumran. Men and women celibates
studied the Jewish Bible, recited the psalms around the
clock and read the writings of holy men. They were
parallel with, but independent of the Jewish priesthood.
The Essenes desired to purify Temple worship as they
awaited the Messiah. They practiced ritual bathing and
baptism of their neophytes. They are fairly analogous
with the religious orders of the Church today. Some of
Jesus' disciples, as well as John the Baptist, may have
been a part of the group for a time.

John the Baptist was the charismatic, fiery, gifted
preacher who called sinners to repentance. He per-

formed baptisms of repentance in the Jordan (cf. Lk 3:3ff.). He called himself the forerunner of the greater one to come, whom he identified as Jesus, his cousin, when the latter appeared and asked for baptism (cf. Mt 3:13-17; Mk 1:9-11; Lk 3:21-22). John did not get involved in ritual or doctrine. His moral message was spiritual conversion of heart.

There is a similarity between some of the themes of John the evangelist and the Essenes. This discovery was disclosed from the Dead Sea scrolls, found in the caves that flank the ruins of the Essenes' monastery today. Peter and Andrew, at their first contact with Jesus, were probably disciples of John the Baptist before they followed the Master to Galilee, where they were definitely chosen as apostles.

Then Jesus began to generate a following as well. Scribes, Pharisees and even some priests came from Jerusalem to investigate the spiritual revolution taking place near the Jordan. Scribes were analogous with canon lawyers today and Pharisees were like the moral theologians. They considered themselves interpreters of religious law and custom. Some asked John for his baptism, but he did not hesitate to call them a *"brood of vipers"* (Mt 3:7).

Jesus himself was only one of many itinerant rabbis who lived on alms and slept wherever anyone offered a bed. As they traversed Palestine, these itinerant rabbis permitted only the smartest applicants to be their close followers. They claimed the "inside track" with God. The priests of the Temple were, of course, the liturgical and ritual experts of Judaism, as well as the dogmatic theologians.

We are not surprised by the antagonism of some against Jesus. But it is most startling to hear that John the Baptist's disciples were critical of Jesus, too. In today's reading, there was some disagreement over the rite of purification, but the real issue is that John's followers were gravitating to Jesus. Jealousy was the motivation of the disciples of the Baptist who approached him about Jesus. They did not want their idol, the Baptist, to be replaced by Jesus, nor have it appear that they themselves had "hitched their wagon to a falling star."

John beautifully compared himself to a groom's *"best man"* who stands up to a marriage. The Baptist was glad to play "second fiddle" to the groom, Jesus. What a remarkable testimony to John's humility. He let go of his own followers to send them to Jesus. *"He must increase; I must decrease."* This is the bottom line of all spiritual growth. John teaches us not to be possessive of our own viewpoints and ideas. *"Be on your guard against idols,"* St. John says in the last line of the first reading today.

Rigidity of opinion soon murders the conscience. Evil is never perpetrated with such gusto and conviction, someone wrote, as when it is done in the name of religion. "Holy Wars," persecution of heretics and fanaticism of every sort have been perpetrated throughout history. Fixation on one's ideas gives the appearance of unswerving loyalty to one's ideals; it justifies any action and rationalizes every evil. When the banner of fanaticism is raised, all reason cedes to feeling as the battle is joined for people's allegiance. True religion, instead, must be the victory of persuasion over coercion. Faith, of course, is always the free gift of God and is apart from religion as such.

Some people within the Church herself stoop to labeling and name-calling in a spirit of divisiveness. Yet Christ is one. His Body must remain united under one head in heaven and on earth, with the Holy Spirit as its soul. Frankly, that generally means that the individual must decrease so that Christ's Body, greater than the mere sum of its parts, can increase.

Sunday after January 6
The Baptism of
the Lord, A, B, C

Is 42:1-4, 6-7;
Acts 10:34-38;
(A) Mt 3:13-17;
(B) Mk 1:7-11;
(C) Lk 3:15-16, 21-22

Today's feast of the Lord's baptism is a "bridge" Sunday. It marks the end of the Christmas cycle and is the beginning of the Sundays of Ordinary Time. This cycle, in turn, will be interrupted by Lent and the Easter cycle. Afterwards, Ordinary Time will resume and continue until the end of the liturgical year marked by the feast of Christ the King. It is often helpful to have a mental map of the Church's overall plan.

The baptism of Jesus was certainly unnecessary. John was preaching a baptism of repentance and Jesus had no sins. But the event provided the scene of another epiphany of the Trinity. The first took place at the Annunciation, during which all three Persons of the Trinity were first mentioned in the same passage in the Bible. Jesus' baptism ends this cycle by making another similar statement about the activity of the Trinity. The Annunciation signaled the appearance of the Lord. His baptism marks his "vocation," his public mission, his inauguration.

Matthew (Year A) is always preoccupied with the "Jewishness" of Jesus. His Gospel alternately portrays him as the new Abraham, new Moses, new David and the last prophet. The reading from second Isaiah is the first so-called Suffering Servant Song (of which there are four). Scholars apply them to the whole of Israel as a corporate Messiah, to the Church as the Mystical Body, or to Jesus himself as God's suffering, redeeming servant. (It would be helpful to read all four Songs, which appear between chapters 42 and 53 of Isaiah.)

Speaking in the person of and as the voice of Yahweh, the servant pleases God who confers his Spirit upon him. (Note that this is the same Holy Spirit who hovers over Jesus in the form of a dove in the Gospels of Matthew, Mark, and Luke—because this is an important theological statement.)

Isaiah's Suffering Servant is quiet and gentle, not shouting in the streets. Thus Jesus preferred to broadcast his message rather than himself. The bruised reed is someone who is spiritually weak, injured or handicapped. The Servant will not snap such a reed in two and throw it aside. Nor will he extinguish or stamp out a barely smouldering wick, that is, someone who is falling into sin. Instead he will try to fan the flame of spiritual life. This is surely comforting to us weak and volatile sinners.

The text from the Acts of the Apostles recounts Peter's sermon at the house of the Gentile convert, Cornelius. Peter stresses that God accepts everyone, including the Gentiles. Because Jesus said openly that he was sent to redeem the house of Israel, the vicar of Jesus, St. Peter, had to be prompted by the Holy Spirit and St. Paul to include the Gentiles. Peter points out that God was with Jesus, his beloved Son.

All four gospels narrate the baptism by John in the Jordan River. Certain elements also appear in all four accounts. The Holy Spirit is conferred upon Jesus, although he had the Spirit from his conception in Mary's womb. He is the beloved Son in whom the Father is "well pleased." This is especially emphasized by Luke (Year C). John depicts the Baptist crying out at the sight of Jesus, *"Behold the Lamb of God, who takes away the sin of the world"* (Jn 1:29). This is another obvious reference to the Suffering Servant of Isaiah who wrote that the Servant was silent as a lamb before his shearers.

The theological implication and practical applications of the baptism of the Lord are several: 1) The Holy Trinity is clearly enunciated: the voice of the Father, the baptism of the Son, the Spirit in the form of a dove. The Triune God is involved with the sanctification of all human beings. 2) Jesus makes a self-disclosure: he came to heal and save what was lost, yet in a meek and humble manner. 3) In all four gospels, John admits that he is not worthy to loosen Jesus' sandal straps.

The summary statement, *"He must increase; I must decrease"* (Jn 3:30) is the essence of the spiritual life. We convict ourselves of sin, proclaim our own unworthiness and consequently accept Jesus as our Savior. The program of spiritual growth requires dying to ourselves, curtailing our long distance "ego trips," and "putting on Christ" to replace the "old Adam" in us all. We stop our power ploys, our manipulations of others' lives, the demanding of our real or supposed rights, the pressing of our personal viewpoints. We try, like Jesus, to allow for bruised reeds and barely smouldering wicks and thus become peacemakers.

Finally, the heavenly Father will reach down from heaven, touch us and lift us up and say, "You are my beloved child. On you my favor rests." Just as the Holy Spirit formed Jesus in the Virgin's womb, so he continues to form Jesus within us, increasing him and diminishing us. Thus we ourselves become beacons of light, reflecting the wonderful works of salvation he has wrought in our souls.

Appendix

APPENDIX

Preparation for the Sacrament of Reconciliation, I

Read Is 11:1-10

This reading is probably the most characteristic of Advent. It is, of course, Isaiah, the most poetic of the "literary" prophets (those who actually wrote or whose statements were gathered by their disciples). The present figure of speech is this: a tender floweret, a tiny bud, a small shoot will spring from the *"stump of Jesse."* Jesse was King David's father and David was his youngest son, his small *"shoot."* God speaks to Isaiah to tell his people that a descendant of David, filled with the gifts of the Holy Spirit, would always occupy the throne of Judah. That royal throne would be everlasting—which might appear to be exaggerated, but which, in fact, is absolutely true and literal: the throne of Jesus is eternal.

At the end of the reading we hear: *"The root of Jesse... the Gentiles will seek out."* All this was fulfilled in Christ. Yet this has remained a problem to this very day. Although (through his legal father, Joseph) Jesus was a lineal descendant of David, according to the genealogies of Matthew and Luke, the previous line of royal heirs had died out under King Zedekiah. He had rebelled against the mighty empire of Nebuchadnezzar, ruler of what is now modern Iraq. Jerusalem was demolished. Because King Zedekiah withstood the siege and delayed Nebuchadnezzar's conquest, Zedekiah witnessed his future, his hope—that is, his two sons— slaughtered. Then Zedekiah was blinded and condemned to live out his life in his personal dark prison in Babylon. Thus perished the ruling family of the house of David. That is why Jesse is referred to as a *"stump."* So the Jews must ask, "How is God keeping his promise? There is no davidic throne in Israel." The Hasidic or very orthodox Jews are still awaiting the Messiah, the spiritual offspring of David, to return to Palestine.

What has this to do with the confession of sin, the sacrament of Reconciliation? Precisely this: the Jews of Jesus' time failed to comprehend his intention, the spiritual dimension of his requirements and the spiritual meaning of his promises. We are not to look for an earthly kingdom: money, power, the ability to manipulate others, arrogance, domination of others. As recovering alcoholics put it, "Let go—let God!" This means we should let go of controlling others' lives and give up our ego trips. We should allow God to intervene in our personal histories to bring us into his kingdom.

Examine yourself. Are God's spiritual promises the measure of your life? Are you trying to establish an earthly kingdom for yourself when God's reign lies elsewhere? Are you "making deals" with God to receive favors or are you working rather because it is the right thing to do? Are you giving God one thing (as if you knew what is best), when he is asking you for something else? What sins do you cling to, repeat the most in confession or are reluctant to give up? Prepare for and make this confession as if this were the first confession of your life (with innocence and candor), the only confession of your life (with intensity and fervor and zeal) and the last confession of your life (with complete thoroughness and honesty).

Preparation for the Sacrament of Reconciliation, II

Read Eph 4:17-32

Italians and the English, as well as other nationalities, have the custom of setting up the Christmas crib scene. The stable with the Holy Family, angels, shepherds and kings is set within a typical village environment. The charming Italian *presepio* shows the villagers shopping, chatting, partying, working at their chores, dancing, nursing babies and so forth. Our Christian instinct is to stress that the enfleshed Word dwelt among us and was like us in all things but sin.

Jesus' involvement with us was complete. His love affair with mankind is perpetual. Although the essential work of redemption was complete, Jesus so loved his human nature and his share in our lives that he kept his human nature when he ascended into heaven. When he said at his Ascension that we should preach the Gospel to all creation (cf. Mk 16:15), he seems to imply all of nature—even inanimate creation. St. Francis of Assisi wrote a Canticle of Creatures by which to praise God. Of course, chapter 4 of Ephesians explains that our human relationships with each other are the priority.

Examine, therefore, how you relate—first to God, because he is the main Person in our lives, then to one another. Examine yourself in specific ways as a spouse, parent, friend, neighbor, employee, student, club member. Do you really struggle for sobriety, chastity, the spirit of prayer? Do you make time for others?

How do you use the world's resources and even the amount of money and property committed to your care? Are "things" a support or a hindrance to your spiritual growth? Are you "baptizing" the visible world by serving and praising God better? Or do you exploit the earth selfishly?

Jesus understands failure. In worldly eyes, he might himself have been considered a failure. He was deserted, betrayed, denied by the disciples and executed as a criminal. He was buried in another man's grave, apparently to be forgotten and put down by his enemies. Therefore Jesus understands the "real" world with its vicissitudes and problems.

Sometimes it helps to compare what Jesus and his family might have endured in similar circumstances in our own day. Someone once wrote a story that goes more or less like this:

A young couple had to go away from home on a necessary business trip. The wife was pregnant and the trip was bumpy in their battered old pickup truck. It was a cold December night when the truck broke down. At the same time, with all the excitement, the woman felt that her time to give birth was fast approaching.

The couple looked for the cheapest motel in town, because that was all they could afford, but the motels and hotels were all filled with travelers. Besides, no one wanted the woman to give birth under his or her roof. And there was no hospital in town. The husband desperately sought a gas station where he could look in the yellow pages for a doctor in town. He could also buy a part for the truck, which by now was barely limping along and kept stalling.

The station owner was about to close up and the regular mechanic was long gone. Meanwhile the woman began her labor. The owner, seeing her plight, let her take shelter in the back garage. So she delivered her baby with the minimal heat of a pot-bellied stove and amid the odors of gas and machinery. Then the best she could do was put her baby in a cardboard carton which served as a crib.

Imagine, if you can, that this garage birth became the focus and turning point of world history.

Jesus has shared our human condition. Yes, he is part of the family. He shared our sinful condition without sin of his own. If we give him the pieces of our broken life in the sacrament of Reconciliation, he will put us back together again.

Preparation for the Sacrament of Reconciliation, III

Read Jn 1:6-28

Literature professors tell their college students that a successful drama or novel calls for character development and, in fact, a change in the lead character. At a time of the year when we see Charles Dickens' *A Christmas Carol* televised, we can observe this process in a moving way. Even though the Christ Child—the "reason for the season"—is never mentioned once, *A Christmas Carol* is a wonderful Christmas story. With the pressure of sending cards, wrapping gifts and decorating, we all can have a little Scrooge in us. Sometimes I feel sympathetic to old Ebenezer, who said, "Everyone who celebrates Christmas should be boiled in his own plum pudding and buried with a sprig of holly through his heart."

By the end of the story, however, we rejoice at the triumph of charity and Scrooge's "conversion." He made reparation to those whom he had wronged (which is essential to real sorrow for sin), went through a character change and learned to keep Christmas better than anyone in London. Even if we are not quite as wicked as Scrooge, we can all stand a little character change to put a happy ending on the story of our lives. "Happy endings" cheer us and lift others up in spirit. We rejoice over Tiny Tim's cure, the defeat of the Mouse King in the Christmas fantasy, the "Nutcracker Suite" and Cinderella's wedding to the prince.

During Sunday and weekday liturgies, we have been quoting both Isaiah and John the Baptist to make straight the Lord's way into our hearts. Obviously, that is meant in a figurative sense. It is our lives that are crooked and our virtues that need deepening.

If we were to eliminate one sin a year from our lives, after just ten years we would be top-of-the-line, state-of-the-art, true-blue Christians. What is a saint, if not one who has converted to the Lord with profound character change for the better? Never say that you are too selfish to change, that you can't bring yourself to love a certain person or that a particular sin is "second nature to me now." Of course, you can't do it alone, but let the Good Shepherd be your guide and the Holy Spirit your Advocate. We may experience ignorance of spiritual truths and lack of conviction that we belong to God's kingdom. Our difficulty may be spiritual and emotional sicknesses, such as loneliness, depression or guilt. Our shepherd-king pursues us into the dark recesses of our souls, the corners of our fantasy life, our twisted ways of thinking and acting. Now is the acceptable time. Now is the moment to submit to God's grace in the sacrament of Reconciliation.

SP **St. Paul Book & Media Centers:**

Alexandria, VA
Anchorage, AK
Boston, MA
Charleston, SC
Chicago, IL
Cleveland, OH
Dedham, MA
Edison, NJ
Honolulu, HI
Los Angeles, CA
Miami, FL
New Orleans, LA
New York, NY
King of Prussia, PA
San Antonio, TX
San Diego, CA
San Francisco, CA
St. Louis, MO
Staten Island, NY
Toronto, Ontario, CANADA

False on God's agenda.

P. 18